Masterpieces of Americana

The Collection of
Mr. and Mrs. Adolph Henry Meyer

Text by Joan Barzilay Freund

SOTHEBY'S BOOKS
New York • London

Dedicated to Jess and Grace Pavey

The Publisher wishes to thank the following individuals
for their generous assistance in the preparation of
this book: Barbara Meyer Livy, Jonathan Meyer Thomas,
Mike McPhee, William Ramsey of the Whittier Trust
Company of Nevada, and Jeanne Arnold, Tim Balboni,
Amy Todd, Cathy McCullough, Annabelle Brown and
Kristina Bogojavlensky of Sotheby's. Our appreciation
to Joan Romano and Katherine Behrens.

The Publisher and the Meyer family also wish to
thank Leslie Keno, Director of the American Furniture
Department at Sotheby's, for his extraordinary
contribution.

SOTHEBY'S BOOKS
New York • London
Director: Ronald Varney
Executive Editor: Signe Warner Watson
Associate: Annabelle Brown

The attributions in this book are based upon current scholarship
and are subject to change based upon new information and future
research.

PHOTOGRAPHS BY:
Dirk Bakker: pages 6, 15, 16, 17, 19, 20, 21, 24, 25, 28, 29, 30, 36,
40, 43, 44, 48, 49, 53, 55, 56, 57, 58, 59, 62, 63, 66, 67, 68, 71, 74,
75, 76, 77, 79, 80, 81, 82, 83, 84, 85, 86, 87, 88, 89, 90, 91, 92, 93.

Ben Cohen: pages 3, 4, 18, 20, 22, 23, 24, 26, 27, 28, 31, 32, 33,
34, 35, 41, 42, 45, 46, 52, 54, 60, 61, 64, 65, 70, 72, 73, 78.

Peter Harholdt: cover, pages 37, 38, 39.

DESIGNED BY:
Timothy Balboni and Jeanne Arnold

Printed in Hong Kong

Contents

Introduction

    Wendell Garrett   5

    Graham Hood   12

Seventeenth Century Furniture   14

Queen Anne Furniture   21

Chippendale Furniture   41

Federal Furniture   71

Folk and Decorative Art and Furniture   85

Endnotes   95

Rendezvous with Destiny: The Meyer Collection

Wendell Garrett

Adolph and Ginger Meyer

The 1930s were a time of ongoing transitions and severe shocks, of economic and political issues linked with the Great Depression and the New Deal, of rising fears of fascism and totalitarianism, and the darkening clouds of war. Other themes that hold pride of place in any examination of the thirties must include the shifting patterns in the power and distribution of industries, the vivid saga of labor organization, and the multifaceted story of agricultural change with the massive migration of down-and-out families and single people looking for work, food, and shelter. While the depression in the United States and impending war overseas sharpened the consciousness of the breakup of unified traditions and fixed principles in America and provided ample cause during the 1930s for fears of collapse and disorder, or peril both domestic and foreign, some of these same events and ideals rested on a desire for permanent truths, a commitment to values long established, stimulating Americans to look single-mindedly toward the past—the colonial past. In the face of daunting challenges and unresolved contradictions that marked the decade, Americans struggled earnestly to hold onto meanings from their past and to see themselves, with all their multiplicity and pluralism, as a single people moving forward in time. In 1936 President Franklin Roosevelt caught something of this sense of exceptionalism and historical mission in his second nomination acceptance speech when he ended with these climactic sentences: "There is a mysterious cycle in human events. To some generations much is given. Of other generations much is expected. This generation of Americans has a rendezvous with destiny."

In this era of fragmentation and change, Adolph Meyer and Ida (Ginger) Schuart Meyer began to collect American art and antiques. Directly and indirectly, consciously and by happenstance, they shaped and were shaped by the fundamental assumptions and ideas of unity, stability, and cohesiveness of a "traditional America." American antiques were the answer in an effort to make sense of the world. Adolph Meyer wrote in 1953 to the pre-eminent American antique furniture dealer, Israel Sack, on the importance of preserving American heritage: "While we are not as old as France and do not have such an historic counterpart as Versailles, we do have 'All the Glories that are America' and an awakening appreciation of our own pioneer creative spirit as well as examples of our own classics also developed in the eighteenth century." Meyer with other Americans found the historical past comfortable and dependable. The tendency to look wistfully backward was reinforced by the powerful and pervasive

An oil painting of an early Territorial Governor of Michigan, George Bryan Porter, painted by Jacob Eicholtz, circa 1830, is one of the most historically important paintings in the Meyer collection.

painters (Thomas Hart Benton and Grant Wood). American materials were also at the center of music in the theme of rural patriotism, as a number of composers sought to make their music specifically expressive of the culture of the United States. Virgil Thomson relied on American hymns and songs in writing the scores for the documentary films *The Plow That Broke the Plains* and *The River*, and drew on the Cajun songs of the bayou for his score of the film *Louisiana Story* (1948). Aaron Copland, seeking to reach a broad audience by expressing himself musically in what he regarded as the "simplest possible terms," drew on native songs and multiple American traditions in such works as *Billy the Kid* (1938) and *Our Town* (1940) and used variations on Shaker songs and country fiddle tunes to capture Pennsylvania rural life in *Appalachian Spring* (1944). Many Americans encountered these pastoral images in the genre of musical films offering viewers the illusion of Norman Rockwell's America: a family-centered and largely traditional world frozen in time in *Meet Me in St. Louis* (1944), *State Fair* (1945), *The Harvey Girls* (1946), and *Summer Holiday* (1948). This 1940s mass culture enthusiasm for the sentimental, pastoral musical was a response to wartime separations and disruptions. The mass-market magazines were also in the vanguard of this antiurban ruralism movement, tempting the subdebs with gingham plaids and ruffled blouses and calling on their parents to adopt an "indigenous, honest, straightforward, functional architecture" of the ranch house based on Frank Lloyd Wright's "Prairie Style." The desire to reside in this mythic past was forged during World War II out of a certain wariness of technology and of a long-term American hostility to the city.

impact of technological innovations and revolutionary changes in the mass production of consumer goods, by art deco skyscrapers and futuristic cityscapes, and in the "jazz moderne" style in everything from radios to dinnerware. New forms of communication—the radio and the telephone—became available for the first time, and electric power for illumination and for driving machines of all sorts entered the daily lives of the multitudes in this period. Equally powerful for the middle class and the wealthy was their ambivalent attitude toward all the futuristic machine-age gear and design with a yearning for the colonial past that they thought simpler and more comforting. Images of rural small towns and lush cultivated farms of harmony and unity coexisted with a new world wholly committed to the futuristic visions and skills of engineers and designers. But on a deeper cultural level, for millions of Americans still out of work and suffering the social and economic realities of depression America, science and technology had not proven to be the boon they had promised to be; the decade-long misery was hardly an indication of the human race's best efforts at planning and managing. By the thirties advertisers were promoting the traditional as much as they were hawking the new.

With nationalism as a guiding theme, various expressions of a heightened interest in local, regional, folk, and ethnic cultures during the thirties appeared as emblems of a depression-inspired urge toward national self-discovery in the paintings of urban realists (Edward Hopper and Charles Burchfield) and the midwestern regionalist

Adolph Meyer was born on February 16, 1893, in Detroit, Michigan, the son of a German immigrant craftsman. Raised in an austere German-speaking household, he dropped out of school at the age of fifteen to begin an apprenticeship in the engineering department of the Packard Motor Car Company, the premium brand and at the pinnacle of automotive status at that time, and advertised as "the standard of the world . . . serving America's aristocracy." As a teenager he maintained a disciplined routine of thrift, industry, initiative, dependability, and the dream of success, continuing his formal education at night school and through correspondence courses. After nine years as an automotive apprentice, he joined the United States Army for two years during World War I. After the war, he returned to Packard in the sales and engineering department, where he worked for the next decade until he was thirty-six. Shortly after resuming his work at the company, he married Ida (Ginger) M. Schuart, and a year later, their only child, Barbara, was born.

In 1936, in the midst of the Great Depression, Meyer, at the age of forty-three, founded the American Screw Products Company in Farmington, Michigan, a manufacturer of finely machined metal products. Then in 1945 at the close of World War II, he established the Vulcan Forging Company in Dearborn, manufacturing connecting rods for automobile engines built by the Ford Motor Company. Living frugally for fourteen years in a small rented apartment with his wife and daughter, through the ethic of hard work, steady accumulation of wealth, and prudent and limited expenditure, Meyer was finally able to purchase a fine house with his savings of $28,000, which would serve his family as their primary residence for the next forty years.

Adolph Meyer at the ground-breaking ceremonies of the Vulcan Forging Company, July 1, 1955, and to the right, construction begins.

The automobile—probably the most powerful American icon of the twentieth century—became a necessity rather than a luxury for most Americans after World War II and Meyer's Vulcan Forging Company prospered enormously as a consequence. Postwar Americans threw aside their wartime, group-based culture of production—assembly lines, factories, and mass production—for a culture of consumption in which the American male in particular exhibited a profound fascination with the automobile. Jack Kerouac's account of his adventures and travels around the country in 1948 appeared in 1957 in the appropriately titled Beat classic *On the Road*. Amid this car craze and love of speed in the late 1940s, aviation-derived concepts of airflow, "torpedo" and "teardrop" shapes, chromed cascade grilles, and aeronautical tail fins were parts of the streamlining aesthetic worked out aerodynamically in wind tunnels by engineers and industrial designers for the up-to-date car.

The thirties Americans produced a spate of popular references to the "American Way of Life" and "The American Dream." But in the 1930s there was by contrast also a mood of romanticization of indigenous societies found in their folk materials—an examination, stimulated by the depression, of the lowbrow world of the vernacular and folk art as opposed to the highbrow world of intellect and experience. Constance Rourke in *American Humor* (1931) presented evidence that the foundations of American literature and art lay among the people, and could be found with its roots in folk humor, in the overlapping comic traditions of Yankee, backwoodsman, and minstrel, and made a case for the worthiness of a national tradition based on folk sources. What made American national character American, she argued, was the culture of the folk in all its legend-creating and myth-making fertility, in all its practical and decorative inventiveness. Having helped organize a folk festival in St. Louis, Rourke became the first editor of the *Index of American Design* in 1936. Made possible by the inventiveness of New Deal relief efforts, the *Index* put artists to work across the country seeking out and preparing careful drawings of American arts and crafts—textiles, silver, furniture, pottery, and the like. Ultimately, some 20,000 examples of these folk materials chosen from the drawings became part of the *Index*, demonstrating the creativity and imagination of the common people.

Cultural historians of the 1930s and 1940s devoted a great deal of attention to what they called "grass-roots history." It was at this time that Henry Ford, the automobile industrialist—who had a curious attitude toward the past and talked of reading decorative arts books—established his historical museum and village in Dearborn, Michigan, because he "wanted to preserve what he appreciated as the contribution of the plain men who never got into history." Ford, the completely self-assured automotive pioneer who often exhibited a narrow materialism, utilitarianism, and anti-intellectualism in fields for which he was ill-equipped, is now famous for the perverse three-word aphorism: "History is bunk." Obviously he was referring to schoolbooks, which, he remembered, "began and ended with wars." After 1932, when Ford spent less time on company affairs, the outside project which absorbed most of his time was Greenfield Village (named for Greenfield Township, his birthplace), a rather idiosyncratic living-history museum, looking backwards to a rural landscape and depicting the lives of middle-income Protestants in an agrarian setting and memorializing their values. Ford now had a fruitful new mission in life. "I'm going to start up a museum and give people a true picture of the development of the country," he told Ernest Liebold, his principal secretary. "That's the only history that is worth observing, that you can preserve within itself. We're going to build a museum that's going to show industrial history, and it won't be bunk."

The concept of history as objects and exhibits rather than words in books was at least as old as the tombs of Egypt, but it seems to have struck Ford suddenly, and his interest in historical artifacts expanded rapidly. As his concept of history matured, it included an appreciation and study of "the general resourcefulness of our people" and he decided to collect "all American things—domestic and mechanical." He came as close to doing this as one man ever will. History included last year's steam locomotives and last week's airships, the growth of the country through industry, achievements with tools and machines. Ford's collections in his living-history museum at Dearborn were arranged in five "impressive, dignified, in every way very satisfying" new buildings and were notable and voluminous in the following classifications: farm implements and machinery, mines and metallurgy, household and kitchen furniture, domestic utensils, costumes, recreation and amusements, lighting, spinning,

weaving, sewing, trade and commerce, timekeeping, medicine and surgery, communication and record of ideas, music, photography, science, schools, taverns, peddlers and chapmen, maps and pictures, fire prevention, forestry and woodworking, horticulture, machine tool and shop practice, steam traction engines and, of course, transportation. (Only one major activity of man was slighted—there were no weapons or mementos of war.) The Henry Ford / Greenfield Village / Edison Institute complex at Dearborn lives on in the vast collections and the more than 100 buildings with a basic purpose of education. The Museum exhibits classified arts, tools, machines, and products; the Village arranges them in historic houses and old workshops (including fifty-one "transplanted originals") in ways they were once used and lived with; and the Institute is a school. It is ironic that the two largest and most popular living-history museums—depicting rural "peaceable kingdoms" that tended to ignore conflict and infused the re-created historical setting of working farms with nostalgia—were sponsored by prominent industrialists, champions of mechanization and mass production, John D. Rockefeller, Jr., at Colonial Williamsburg and Henry Ford in Greenfield Village. As Americans' faith in the old deepened and they struggled to hold onto meanings from their past, the feeling that American antiques were important not only because of their aesthetic qualities, but also their historical associations, became firmly rooted.

The most brutal and deadly war in the world's history ended in 1945, and Americans turned to peace with an almost desperate self-consciousness. The very titles of some motion picture films—*It's a Wonderful Life*, *The Best Years of Our Lives*, *The Time of Your Life*, and *Living in a Big Way*—suggest the high level of awareness with which this project of "living" was pursued. The new President, Harry Truman, went to the final conference of the allied leaders in Potsdam with the attitude of a gunslinger who was convinced he was quicker on the draw. Truman's tough vetoes, combative liberalism, and ability to present himself as the "symbol of the real virility of his party" won him the 1948 election. Now began the American century, or so he and many others thought. The next wave of outdoor history museums by the 1950s included the New York State Historical Association's Farmer's Museum in Cooperstown (Stephen Carlton

Clark, Sr., heir to the Singer Sewing Machine fortune); Old Sturbridge Village (the Wells brothers of the American Optical Company) and Historic Deerfield (Henry J. Flynt) in Massachusetts; Old Salem in North Carolina; Mystic Seaport in Connecticut; and the Shelburne Museum in Vermont (Electra Havemeyer Webb), all preserved or re-created outdoor communities more modest than Williamsburg or Greenfield Village. There were also Winterthur Museum (Henry Francis du Pont of the Delaware chemical fortune); the Garvan collection at Yale University (Francis Patrick Garvan); and the Bayou Bend collection at the Museum of Fine Arts, Houston (Ima Hogg, Texas oil and real estate). As the historic sites and decorative arts museums grew, the quest for colonial antiques nationwide became an obsession in these early cold war years—an age of doubt and anxiety colored by the atomic bomb and international communism, by rampant commercialism and the UFO scare. The history of an earlier, rural, pre-industrial nation became a safe mooring for many Americans, but it was a nostalgic vision of an idealized past that never happened so clearly or existed so nobly. The three-dimensional *Better Homes and Gardens* inspirational version of historical settings and lifestyles re-created at these various living-history museums, which showed visitors how a community worked, tended to downplay aspects of community life that were dysfunctional and/or produced conflict and strife, ignoring violence, vigilantism, family discord, labor conflict, insects and smells, slave auctions, and minority political movements. In this postwar era, it was the inspiration of these attractive and appealing objects from the early American home life that attracted Adolph and Ginger Meyer as collectors. With the Vulcan Forging Company prospering following World War II, the Meyers were now in a financial position to afford what would become their lifelong passion—the collecting of American furniture that was artistically successful—American antiques that were links to a rich cultural past.

The Meyers were a formidable pair, with Adolph's business drive and attention to detail coupled with Ginger's exquisite taste, not only in her clothing and everything she designed, but also from the exceptional decor and furnishings in her home to her prize-winning garden which became a regular stop on garden club tours.

Despite a manufacturing career in the production of metal products, Adolph Meyer had a lifelong appreciation for woodworking, particularly fine furniture, since his father had been an Old World cabinetmaker before emigrating to America. It was the father, in fact, who, having worked in near servitude as a craftsman for the European aristocracy, instilled in his son the value of free artistic expression as could be found only in America; he felt that there was enshrined in the forms of furniture used by the earliest settlers a spirit not found in the exotic shapes and decoration that came from England and Europe. He loved and appreciated American antiques as examples of genuine art because they embodied the strength and beauty in the character of the leaders of American settlement. In looking ardently to the American past for both inspirational and artistic models, Meyer was representative of his generation. Beautiful objects had been made by American craftsmen because of, not in spite of, an egalitarian society, free from the feudal restraints of an established church, entrenched aristocracy, and hereditary monarchy. So with enthusiasm and pride—now that he had the money and the desire to go after the highest-priced

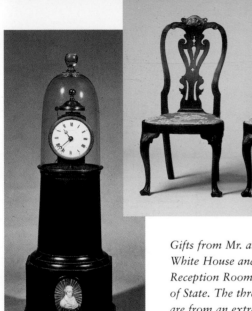

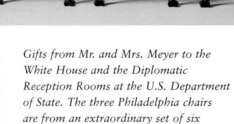

Gifts from Mr. and Mrs. Meyer to the White House and the Diplomatic Reception Rooms at the U.S. Department of State. The three Philadelphia chairs are from an extraordinary set of six donated by the Meyers.

respected dealer and American furniture authority, Jess Pavey of Birmingham, Michigan. They were taught to visually examine and inspect objects and by comparison and contrast note their certain physical properties of material, construction, technique, and condition. Fortified with a good visual memory, the Meyers were taught by Pavey to investigate the "how" and "why": how people made and used particular objects, and why certain objects were fashionable; how the fashionable styles of the past compared with present-day aesthetic responses; and why regional tastes of that day differed from place to place. Pavey taught the Meyers that regionalism distinguished antique objects by construction practices, attitudes of taste, transmission of ideas and designs, and the use of particular local secondary woods that defined regions in early America. If regionalism (or place) was used as one baseline in the triangulation of the difficult terrain of American antiquities by this dealer, periodization (or time) was another important guideline. Among the many reasons for stylistic change in the designs and purposes of objects over time was the power of fashion. The third baseline in triangulating authenticity of antiques was an understanding of craft techniques—the "art and mystery," in the words of Joseph Moxon—of the specific crafts. And it was the subject of the basic tools and processes of the early American crafts that appealed to Meyer. Jess Pavey's insistence upon perfectionism and the integrity of pieces, combined with Israel Sack's investment theory of "good, better, and best" in American furniture would become Meyer's rules for collecting. Pavey, in fact, advised and handled the vast majority of the pieces in the collection: the furniture, the silver, pottery, textiles, and paintings as well. The two families would become close friends, and eventually Pavey would be appointed to the Board of the Americana Foundation.

During the 1950s and 1960s the Meyers made important contributions of furniture and art to the collections of the White House and to the United States Department of State Diplomatic Reception Rooms, both of which are among the finest displays of Americana in the country. They also made significant contributions to The Henry Ford Museum, the Edison Institute, The Metropolitan Museum of Art, the Detroit Institute of Arts, the Archives of American Art, and various social organizations in

American antiques—Meyer's proclivity to purchase only the very best coupled with his wife's high cultural and artistic standards, enabled them to collect and build a magnificent collection of Americana which was to achieve much well-deserved fame and influence from coast to coast. Along with many other collectors of his generation, Meyer felt that machine-made furnishings lacked grace and taste. Because Adolph Meyer exemplified the work ethic of the American Dream, he began collecting only the finest examples of hand craftsmanship made by hardworking American craftsmen during a time when the national quest for liberty and the rights of man were paramount.

The Meyers were guided in their never-ending quest and all-consuming passion for artifacts by a highly

Michigan. Through a life of hard work, frugality, and tenacity, Adolph and Ginger Meyer used their prosperity to build one of the finest private collections of antique American furniture and other decorative arts. Late in their lives, the Meyers chose to perpetuate their vision of America—a country built on freedom and liberty for all—by establishing and funding the Americana Foundation on December 22, 1960, to encourage and celebrate the American way of life. The application for a tax-exempt status stated the specific purposes for which the Foundation was formed: "The purposes of the Americana Foundation are to receive contributions from donors; to maintain a principal fund; and to use such fund or the income therefrom solely for charitable, educational or scientific purposes by making contributions of funds or of authentic objects of American art to other exempt charitable, educational or scientific organizations, or to the United States of America, a state or possession or a political subdivision of any state or possession for exclusively public purposes; all in the interests or aiding in the preservation of authentic American art." In its first year the Foundation donated an important Simon Willard lighthouse clock and a rare Federal mahogany settee with four matching chairs to the White House collection. In 1962 the Foundation donated a Federal mahogany dining table to the White House at the request of the First Lady, Jacqueline Kennedy, to which gift the Kennedys responded graciously to the Meyers with an invitation to attend a state dinner at the White House and dine at their table. Originally established in New York City, the Foundation was moved to Michigan in 1969. Beginning in 1971, Adolph and Ginger Meyer donated many valuable gifts of American furniture to the Diplomatic Reception Rooms and Curator Clement E. Conger up until their respective deaths in 1980 and 1979. From 1975 until his death, Adolph H. Meyer was a member of the Fine Arts Committee of the Department of State to which his grandson, Jonathan M. Thomas, has recently been appointed.

Striving for the highest standards in everything that interested him, Meyer's passion and drive included his love for animals, particularly the family's pet German shepherd dogs. Learning about the breed and setting out to establish a breeding kennel, he imported a grand champion bitch from Germany and purchased a small, typical

Jess and Grace Pavey with two of the Meyers' grandchildren, Katherine and Jeffrey.

Michigan farm with a farmhouse for raising dogs in the country. Meyer later determined that the farm was part of an original land grant of a quarter section of 160 acres, a tract of land half a mile square, made to Samuel Basset by the United States Government in 1831, which remained in the same family for 120 years until it was purchased by Meyer. In his historical quest and in his demand for excellence, Meyer spent a considerable amount of time and money reassembling the farm which comprised the original land grant made to Basset, and restored the original house and outbuildings, built in 1840 and later, to their original condition. Although the farm and its buildings had been purchased to be used primarily as a kennel for his dogs, in his final years the site, which came to be known as Tollgate, represented to Meyer an important part of America's heritage and culture, and he later authorized grants to Michigan State University and Oakland Community College to operate the farm as "a place for public agricultural education" and asked for a commitment from them to "operate the farm as a learning center."

Few of us live life as abundantly as Adolph and Ginger Meyer did. Through the legacy of the Americana Foundation, we can appreciate today their intellect, their unerring eye, their genuine patriotism, and the strength of their dedication to those things that man creates that make our world better and more beautiful. Without question, they had a "rendezvous with destiny." ★

A Recollection of the Meyers

Graham Hood

Adolph Meyer at dinner with pioneer collector Katherine Prentis Murphy, Donald Shelley, the former director of The Henry Ford Museum and Greenfield Village, and Grace Pavey with her back to the camera.

I met Bob and Ginger Meyer the fall of 1968 when I took the position of curator of American Art at the Detroit Institute of Arts. They were curious—like many others in the community—to meet this young Englishman who was so captivated by American arts that he had devoted his professional career to the field. It wasn't long after my arrival that word of their superb collection reached me, and soon after that I had the privilege of the first of several visits to their home.

I strongly suspect that it was Jess Pavey who made the initial introduction. Having been a dealer in American arts in this region for many years, possessing a shrewd sense of ambition and a strong moral sense about the collecting of American arts (especially those that were "still in the dirty rough"), Jess had played a major role in the development of a number of collections in the Birmingham and Bloomfield Hills areas. I gathered that the Meyers had acquired a number of important pieces from Jess or from Israel Sack on Jess's recommendation.

Though it was 27 years ago, I still have a picture in my mind's eye of entering the Meyers' front hall for the first time and seeing two low-case pieces with block and shell fronts; perhaps one was Connecticut; perhaps both were Newport. It didn't matter, they were superb, I thought, and on further investigation the character of the collection was sustained.

It was the kind of assemblage to make an ambitious curator's mouth keep on watering! But I had strong competition in no less than Clem Conger, curator of the State Department Diplomatic Reception Rooms. I, like many regional museum curators of the time, looked upon Clem as an elegant privateer on the high seas of Americana, without deference to local or regional alliances. The better

Ginger Meyer making a charitable dona-
tion. Standing are Donald Shelley and an
associate of The Henry Ford Museum
and Greenfield Village.

One of the great masterpieces of
Massachusetts Chippendale furniture in
the American Wing of the Detroit
Institute of Arts is a Salem bonnet-top
highboy which was donated by the
Meyers in 1968. The museum produced a special brochure acknowledging
Adolph and Ginger Meyer's generosity
and support.

the collection, the more Clem seemed able to concentrate
his armament and the more difficult it became for the
rest of us.

I distinctly remember a luncheon I organized for a few
of the most important collectors in the region—held in the
boardroom of the Detroit Institute of Arts and hosted by
then director Willis F. Woods—when I sat next to Ginger
Meyer. We had a very cordial chat—we always did, for I
sensed that she liked me, and I took to her modesty. She
told me—at least this is how I remember it—that they had
had a phone call recently from the Secretary of State
(I think it must have been Secretary Rogers) to invite them
to a special reception in Washington. Clearly, this was
at Clem's behest, and clearly Bob and Ginger were deeply
flattered. I was crushed. I was outgunned and outma-
neuvered.

I know the Meyers got quite involved in the
Diplomatic Reception Rooms—that was their preroga-
tive—and, I believe they were gracious and generous. Yet,
they were not parsimonious to the struggling young curator of American Art in Detroit. They did make contributions of cash for pieces that I recommended, and they
were generous in opening their home for receptions.

One more memory. I was talking to Albert Sack one
day and the subject of the Meyers came up. Albert took
me aside and said to me, "You know how to get intimate
with Bob?" I immediately became very interested and
said, "No, please tell me." Albert said, "I don't think Bob

particularly cares for receptions and things like that. The
next time you're out there, say to him, 'Bob, what I'd
really most like to do is to go and see your hogs!'"

Albert winked and said, "I sometimes think Bob likes
his hogs as much as his furniture."

Unfortunately, I never had a chance to pursue this star-
tling tactic. I left for another position soon afterward. The
Meyers attended the elegant reception that the Minnets,
the Keenes and the Levitts, among others, held for Gale
and me upon our departure. A little later, Jess Pavey called
me up and said that he had a present for me that Ginger
especially wanted me to have—a charming little nineteenth-century redware pot that I still have on my desk. ★

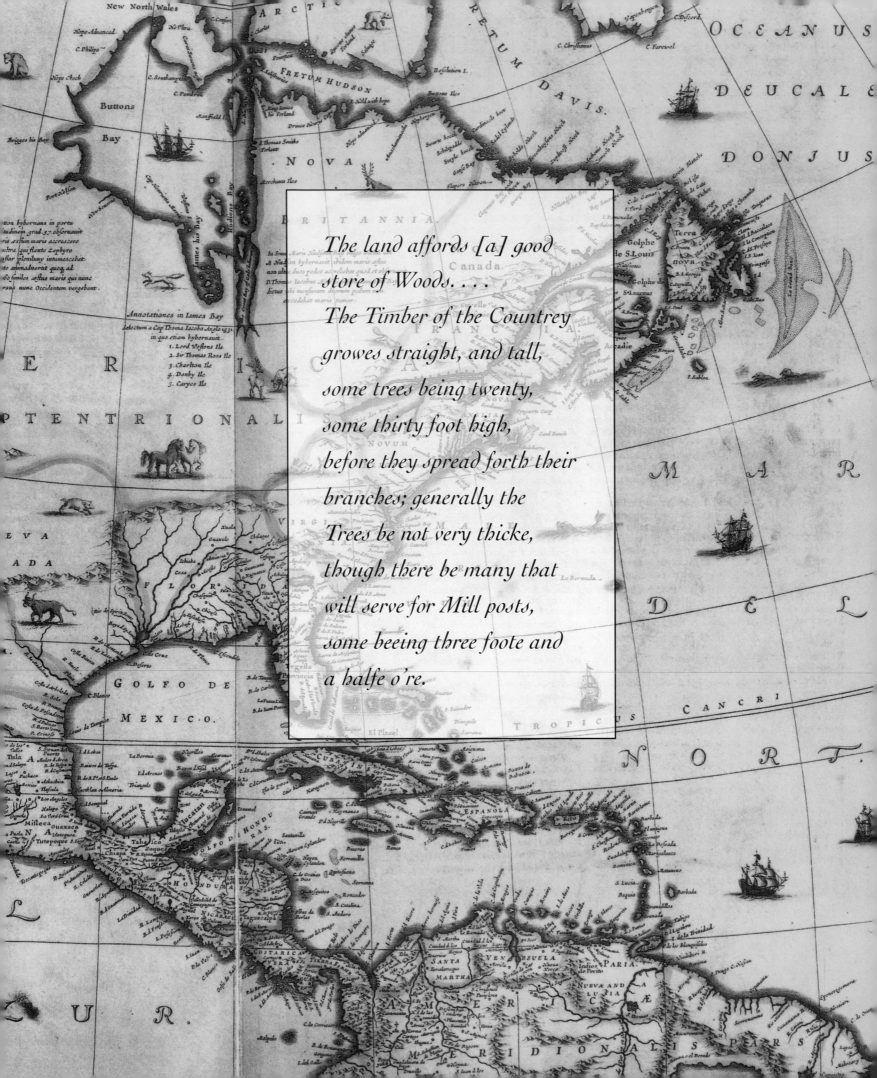

The land affords [a] good
store of Woods. . . .
The Timber of the Countrey
growes straight, and tall,
some trees being twenty,
some thirty foot high,
before they spread forth their
branches; generally the
Trees be not very thicke,
though there be many that
will serve for Mill posts,
some beeing three foote and
a halfe o're.

Seventeenth Century Furniture

So noted William Wood, the appropriately named naturalist, when he visited the Massachusetts colony in 1634. Marveling at the potential of the landscape, he saw opportunity for "an ingenious Carpenter, a cunning Joyner, a handie Cooper, such a one as can make strong ware for the use of the countrie."[1] The furniture which comprises the Adolph H. Meyer Collection, and which is illustrated in the following pages, attests to the wisdom of Wood's observations. In many ways, the scope of these pieces tells the story of the naturalization of foreign artisanship in America.

New England really began to take shape during the period known as the Great Migration, which spanned the years 1630–43. The banks of the Hudson and Connecticut Rivers, Narragansett Bay and Massachusetts Bay offered natural ports and were well positioned to receive the influx of goods and people from abroad. Before many of the nearly 20,000 emigres made the journey from the Old World to the New, they sought advice from a number of broadsides published in London. In one, the Reverend Francis Higginson, the first minister of Salem, Massachusetts, cautioned:

> Before you come . . . be sure to furnish yourself with . . . all manner of carpenters tools and a great deale of iron and steele to make nails, and locks for houses . . . and many other things which were better for you to think of there than to want them here."[2]

Inventories of the earliest New England households contained extensive tool selections, indicating that many of the earliest colonials began as their own carpenters.[3]

By the 1670s the American colonies had grown from "mere outposts" into thriving communities, the most prosperous being Boston, the "Metropolis of New England." The expanding commerce attracted carpenters and joiners

This turned oak "great chair" was made in Massachusetts circa 1680.

This furniture form was an innovation of the late seventeenth century. Previously, storage was provided by chests with hinged tops or large cupboards opening to shelves. The chest of drawers afforded more organized storage as well as a display surface.

The three drawers of this Massachusetts chest, decorated with geometric-paneled designs characteristic of the late seventeenth century, are supported within a joined case with double-paneled ends. Note the lathe-turned ball feet which are evocative of popular European baroque fashion.

who gravitated to the harbor towns where there was ample opportunity for building and furnishing both ships and homes. In addition, the ports provided accessibility to imports: "Hardware and upholstery goods came from England, black walnut from the Middle Colonies, and mahogany from the West Indies."[4]

The earliest piece in the Meyer collection is probably a turned, spindle-back armchair dating from around 1680 (page 15). The form is sometimes called a Carver chair, because a similarly fashioned seat was said to have been brought over on the Mayflower by the first governor of the Plymouth Colony, John Carver. Each finely turned spindle was crafted on a foot-operated pole lathe which spun the lengths of wood while the turner fashioned it into a desired shape with a chisel.[5] Although not a formula, it is generally thought that within the vocabulary of the turner's art, the narrower and more refined the turnings, the later the date of attribution.[6]

In 1716, one wealthy Boston diarist, Samuel Sewall, recalled: "Governour [Samuel] Shute comes to my house in his Chariot, with a petition. . . . Many had Signed it, I signed it in the new Hall; Govr sat in the arm'd Chair."[7] Unknowingly, Sewall underscored the subtext of colonial American seating furniture. Today, the term "chairman" is used to refer to the person who holds the seat of authority because it is derived from the practice of offering a seat to a guest or family leader.[8] There were also, of course, benches, stools and chairs without arms; but a straight-backed chair with armrests, often termed a "great chair," was reserved for persons of privileged position. At mealtimes, the great chair would have been placed at the "head of a family table, at which the seating was strictly ordered according to one's rank within the family hierarchy," while the servants and youngest members of the household were relegated to positions "below the salt." In future generations, the ancestral worth of "great-grandfather's chair" remained strong and as a result, a number of these forms have survived.[9]

Changes on England's political front inevitably inspired surges of stylistic innovation in furniture design. When Charles II ascended the throne in 1660 with his wife, the Portuguese princess, Catherine of Braganza, British craftsmen acquired a taste for the baroque. The previously exiled Charles had been exposed to the art of Holland and

France during his time on the Continent and with his return to the court came a new glamour and a troop of foreign-trained artisans. Moreover, his marriage to Catherine had brought England access to oriental styles and materials thanks to Portugal's trade routes to Bombay, China and the East Indies. James II, the brother and successor to Charles II, was removed from the throne by the Glorious Revolution of 1688, which restored the Stuart monarchy. The Dutch king, William of Orange, and his English wife, Mary Stuart, brought a wave of Netherlandish influences to the court along with the offer of safe haven to the French Huguenot craftsmen who had fled France following the 1685 revocation of the Edict of Nantes.

In England, this period marked a stylistic passage from late-medieval to modern design. Carved decoration took a turn to the ornate as a new fascination with the effects of light and shadow was felt in all the arts. Walnut supplanted oak as the wood of choice because it was more easily carved, lightweight and could be polished to a lustrous finish.[10] Furthermore, the development of dovetailed construction led to a number of new furniture forms. Previous to the dovetail, furniture was constructed of heavy panels of oak which were joined and pegged together within a frame. The flaring structure of the dovetail permitted craftsmen to make cases constructed from a lighter board, usually pine, which could then be sheathed in a decorative wood veneer. The lighter materials made taller pieces possible.

Boston was the first colonial center to support a school of London-educated furniture craftsmen. Just as fashionable folk in London had looked to the Continent for stylistic innovation, the colonies looked to what Samuel Sewall called the far-off "fountain of the English nation."[11] "There is no fashion in London but in three or four months is to be seen in Boston," marveled one visitor to New England in 1700.[12] Certainly this was not always true, however the wealthier colonials sought out new styles because "it was part of their ethic to show their success (evidence of God's favor) and they found craftsmen to make furniture for them that could pass for current on their social and economic level in London."[13]

The geometric decoration of a *circa* 1680 New England chest of drawers has Dutch design roots by way of

Sunlight pouring into the guest bedroom highlights a variety of furniture from the Meyer collection. The New England blue-green-stained maple pencil-post bed is covered in a richly embroidered bedcover, from the same region, detailed on page 15. The Queen Anne mirror above the chest dates to the early eighteenth century. The yellow-grained paint on the early-eighteenth-century New England joint stool was most likely added in the nineteenth century in order to add color to a dimly lit room.

England (page 16). Its architectonic facade is comprised of three long horizontal drawers, each divided into two panels by a bold pattern of turned, applied moldings. Many craftsmen emphasized the surface division with paint; however, after centuries of usage, sunlight and varnish, it is difficult to establish just how strong these colors might have been.[14]

A chest of drawers, rather than a chest with a lidded storage compartment, was an advance in furniture construction which well suited the close quarters of urban living. It was used anywhere, from the bed chamber to the general-purpose space of the hall or parlor. The contents of the drawers might have included textiles, sheets, towels and slipcovers. These fabrics were previously "concealed and protected" in great chests. The chest of drawers made the contents more accessible, as it "flaunted the quantity of textiles therein."[15] One exceptionally detailed 1694 estate inventory from Portsmouth, New Hampshire, described the contents of Ursula Cutt's chest of drawers. It included everything from "8 pair womens glasses and one pair of mens" to an "old pewtr pott" to "Six pair rusty Suzsors." In addition, most case pieces were kept adorned and protected by a draped "cubbard cloth."[16]

The baroque concerns for verticality, the contrast between thick and thin components and the ornamental effects of light upon variegated surfaces are evident in a two-part Massachusetts high chest of drawers dating from around 1710 (left). The burl maple veneer is highly figured and works in place of the applied moldings of the previously pictured chest to enliven the surface. The case has been lifted from the floor on six trumpet- and cup-turned legs which are united by a series of flat, horizontal stretchers designed to mirror the arched pattern of the skirt. The cabinetmaker's decision to support the weighty case piece at the narrowest point of the leg turnings lends a sense of precariousness to the overall scheme. The staggered placement of the escutcheons and hand pulls charges the surface with a shimmering array of highlights. As with the low chest of drawers, this piece would have been used to hold ever-precious linens and cloths. The flat topped pediment provided a display area for "bolles," "China Ware," "alabaster Toys" and other valued bits of memorabilia.[17] ★

LEFT:
This circa 1710 Boston, Massachusetts, *high chest is of unusually small size and is veneered in burled maple over white pine. The drawer fronts are ornamented with the original bright-cut decorated bail brasses and escutcheon plates. In the William and Mary period, high chests of drawers were raised onto six spindly baluster- and trumpet-turned legs. The undulating profile of the skirt is complemented by the flickering surfaces of the figured drawer fronts and case. The curves of the shaped skirt are repeated in the stretchers supporting the legs, adding yet another element of movement to the overall design.*

ABOVE:
Dovetailed case construction allowed for a more lightweight object which could be elegantly veneered with rich and graceful woods.

Queen Anne Furniture

By the early eighteenth century, a ship could sail from London to Boston or New York in six to eight weeks. But the stylistic time lag between American and English furniture was often far greater—sometimes even twenty to thirty years. Edwin J. Hipkiss once observed: ". . . these Anglo-Americans took from England what appeared to them to be admirable and suitable and made it their own."[1] But colonial consumers were not a homogeneous group. American buyers tended to be conservative and demonstrated a taste for traditional forms. They were selective in their adaptation of each successive style that stemmed from London's mercantile or courtly society, and their acceptance was colored by "colonialist sympathies," religious convictions and politics. English furniture was not simply made in the colonies; rather, English style informed American models.[2]

A cabinetmaker gained his knowledge of European style in a number of ways, the most obvious and immediate of which was schooling in London. Many of the new arrivals promoted themselves as fluent in the style "most recent from London" though the essence of their European education was in their minds and hands. Others aspired to merchant status, and bought and sold imported goods to enhance their income. Some colonial craftsmen were requested to repair or duplicate furniture that had been purchased abroad by their clients, while still others looked to printed material in the form of design books or advertisements that served as models for crafted details or entire furniture forms.

Toward the mid eighteenth century, colonial artisans began to respond to the currents of a style which had grown popular in England during the reign of Queen Anne (1702–1714). Walnut remained a favored wood,

LEFT:
Impressive case pieces such as this Boston secretary made circa 1760 are testament not only to the wealth and profession of the owner, but to the practices of society at large. An increasingly literate population had need of a place to store and/or display its books. The arched paneled mahogany doors of this secretary possibly allude to the fact that it was intended for storage and personal use rather than display, otherwise the doors would have been fitted with mullioned panes of glass. The numerous drawers and valanced pigeonholes of the writing interior suggest that the original owner was a businessman or merchant who required space for his records and correspondence.

ABOVE:
The elegance of this English agate-ware teapot was fashionably appropriate for the eighteenth-century pastime of taking tea. Thomas Whieldon, an English ceramacist who entered a partnership with Josiah Wedgwood in Staffordshire in the mid eighteenth century, was particularly well known for his superb aesthetic accomplishment in this medium. Slabs of different colored clay were laid one over the other and were divided and subdivided until they produced the swirling effect which gave this particular ware the name 'agate', after the clouded and swirling colors of the precious stone. Archaeological discoveries support the theory that imported agate-ware was widely popular in certain eighteenth-century American homes.

The fireplace was often the sole provider of warmth. The wings of this plush mid-eighteenth-century Boston easy chair would have captured the glowing warmth of the fire as it flickered across this magnificent Chippendale mahogany piecrust-top tea table from Philadelphia. Above the fireplace hangs an oil painting by Charles Willson Peale of Major John Berrien. An illustration of this painting can be seen on page 53.

This Queen Anne mahogany porringer-top tea table is named for the bold rounded corners of the top which imitate the shape of a porringer (see page 50). Cross braces pierce the side rails beneath the top, a feature characteristic of many Rhode Island tables. The wide overhang of the top is supported by a shallow apron, and delicate vertical legs ending in pad feet offer a sense of frivolity to the very attenuated form.

although imported mahogany gained in popularity among wealthier clients. Case furniture was considered in terms of architectural proportion and informed by decorative motifs stemming from Palladian-based classicism. Seating furniture was ideally characterized by a baroque sensibility featuring sweeping lines, C-scrolls and focused areas of naturalistic ornament.[3] These fashions marked a strong departure from the rectilinear vocabulary of the earlier William and Mary period.

In 1753, William Hogarth, the English painter, termed the serpentine extension of the S-curve, a "line of beauty." He believed that the fluidity of the undulant line "leads the eye a wanton kind of chase, and from the pleasure that gives the mind, entitles it to the name of beautiful."[4] The sometime-satirist used an illustration which paralleled the similarity between the reverse curve and the shape of a woman's corseted torso. Mid-eighteenth-century lasciviousness notwithstanding, it captured the essence of its sensuous sweep.

There were degrees of interpretation of the new sinuosity. Furniture obviously served a variety of purposes, and was made and owned "by all social classes, in both city and country." As such, it served as a barometer of the social makeup and aesthetic values of the nation. American colonial society differed from European models because it was "more uniformly middle-class. . . . And, in this middle-class society, furniture was the most universal art form."[5] The objects with which the colonials surrounded themselves were greatly reflective of their own self-consciousness and social intentions.

The porringer-top table was an all-purpose form that found particular popularity in Rhode Island (left). Its elemental design was light and versatile and served the purposes of solitary dining, gaming, or the taking of tea. The term porringer was a later name attached to the form and stemmed from the similarity of the rounded corners to the shape of a porridge bowl. Porringer tables appear in at least two colonial portraits as supports for the activities of reading and writing: a *circa* 1775 portrait of *Francis and Sanders Malbone* by Gilbert Stuart, and a second, *circa* 1772 portrait of *David Moore* by Samuel King, in which the precarious placement of an inkwell on one turreted table protrusion called attention to the oddity of the form.[6] Meanwhile, in the best of barter traditions, one member of the famed Townsend and Goddard clan of craftsmen, Job Townsend, Jr., traded one cupboard and three porringer-top tables to a customer, who was a barber, in exchange for "A Year's Shaven, A Cutt Wigg, a foretop to the Wigg, and 24 feet of Mahogany."[7]

Now considered an elegant form of living room or parlor furniture, the eighteenth-century "Easie" chair was a form generally intended for use by the elderly or infirm in a bed chamber. Some were even fitted with a commode unit for "nighttime convenience."[8] The shape of the chair was distinguished by a fully upholstered back, wings and armrests, as well as a seat cushion, and evolved from an earlier tradition of reclining invalid chairs.[9] When John Singleton Copley painted a poignant portrait in 1764 of the 82-year-old Anna Susan Dummer Powell seated in an easy chair, he did so to underscore her age.[10] Often upholstered en suite with bed chamber curtains or bed hangings, the easy chair provided a comfortable seat for women during the "lying-in" period of pregnancy.[11]

This circa 1745 Queen Anne easy chair is constructed with walnut pad-foot cabriole front legs, vase- and block-turned stretchers, and maple rear legs characteristic of the Boston Queen Anne style.

As one diarist recalled, a friend who had just given birth was "able the very next day to sit up in her large easy-chair, with her mending basket and book beside her, making first one and then the other her pastime for some hours each day. . . ."[12] The wealthy Philadelphia merchant, John Cadwalader, purchased a large home on Second Street in Philadelphia in 1769 which he and his wife, Elizabeth Lloyd, undertook to renovate the following year. They were great patrons of the Scottish-born craftsman Thomas Affleck, and from him they purchased "2 Mahogany Commode Sophias for the Recesses," "one large ditto" and "an Easy Chair to Sute ditto."[13] This serves as a rare documented instance of a colonial easy chair being made, en suite with parlor furniture. The reason may have been that Elizabeth Cadwalader was of child-bearing age at the time, and "the chair might have been intended for her use."[14]

As the product of a combined effort by an upholsterer and a chairmaker, the easy chair, such as a *circa* 1745 Massachusetts example, was one of the costliest forms of seating furniture (page 25). The Cadwaladers had Affleck deliver his unfinished designs straight to the shop of the upholsterer, Plunkett Fleeson. The day book of another upholsterer, Samuel Grant of Boston, indicated that one-third the cost of the chair went toward the wooden frame and labor while the remaining two-thirds went to the cost of the fabrics and padding materials. The padded form of the chair was crafted by binding and molding the stuffing to conform to the carcass of the frame. Strips of webbing were stretched horizontally and vertically to create a sling within the frame upon which was placed a piece of sack-cloth. A primary stuffing material such as grass was laid upon the sackcloth, "covered with linen and secured with line to both the sackcloth and linen on the seat and simply tied down to the sackcloth back and arms."[15] This structure was then covered with a layer of curled horsehair and linen and ultimately encased within a durable textile to counter the tendency of the stuffing to work through the layers.[16]

Unquestionably, the excellence of colonial Newport furniture design is due to the impact on the trade of the Townsend and Goddard families of cabinetmakers. Although furniture historian Michael Moses has identified sixty-seven Newport craftsmen outside the Goddard-

Among the great masterpieces in the Meyer collection is this magnificent bonnet-top highboy. The highboy reportedly descended in the Gould family of Rhode Island and was purchased for the Meyers by Jess Pavey from a local family who had bought the piece at Du Mouchelle's Auction House in Detroit. The highboy had descended with a stop-fluted Chippendale Newport bedstead which is now in a private collection. Thin sheets of mahogany veneer cover the case just above the knees in order to conceal the dovetails. The mid-molding is attached to the upper case rather than the lower case, a distinctive construction feature almost exclusive to Rhode Island during this period. The detachable angular-edged cabriole legs ending in slipper feet are patterned after a template and glued into the inner edge of the lower case positioned by large pine glue blocks.

Townsend school, the fame of Newport craftsmanship is nevertheless indebted to their reputation.[17] Much of that renown has centered around the blockfront form which reached its stylistic pinnacle about 1780 and is best exemplified by a blockfront mahogany bureau table attributed to Edmund Townsend (page 46). However, an earlier example of a bonnet-top high chest dating from *circa* 1760 serves as a refined expression of Newport's Queen Anne style (page 26).

The high chest is formed of two parts, with the walnut case structure artfully balanced upon squared, cabriole legs ending in slipper feet. During the Queen Anne period, Newport craftsmen fashioned the cabriole leg with either a slipper or pad foot, but the combination of a bonnet-top chest with a slipper foot was rare. A more common occurrence was for craftsmen to team slipper feet with a flat-top chest. In this instance, the line of the cabriole leg was

ABOVE:
All of the characteristics of the fully-developed Philadelphia Queen Anne style are represented in this walnut balloon-seat side chair. Its rhythmic flow and sensual curves illustrate the era's preference for the S-shaped line. This line extends through the profile of the splat, echoing the natural curves of the human body. The development from a trapezoidal seat to a balloon-shaped seat resolved the conflict of conjoining a straight edge with the curve of the cabriole leg and rounded crest rail.

RIGHT:
Leg detail of the Philadelphia walnut balloon-seat side chair shown on page 20

FAR RIGHT:
Back detail of the walnut balloon-seat side chair shown above

Aside from their obvious aesthetic qualities, fire screens served the practical purpose of blocking and capturing the otherwise uneven heat of the open fire. Fire screens were either handheld or raised on poles such as this circa 1760 Boston, Massachusetts, example. Eliza Leslie remarked in her 1840 publication entitled The House Book: or a Manual of Domestic Economy *that embroidered screens could be made "very handsome by a young lady of good taste and well-skilled in drawing." Evidently, such was the case for this lovely embroidered screen, depicting a shepherdess tending her flock in a wreath of vines and flowers.*

incorporated into the skirt in an exquisite manner. The shape of the slipper acted as a device through which the perspective of the form was integrated. Beginning with the narrow point of the toe, the surface was divided in two by the squared treatment of the front legs and merged into the three outer planes of the casepiece through the extension of the visible lines.[18]

The character of the high chest was manifest in the quality of the cabriole legs. In this instance, the slenderness of the legs belies the weight of the towering case piece above. Furthermore, the chest is simply adorned with a carved recessed shell embedded in the apron and the central finial in the bonnet-top, which has been replaced. The original finial probably had a cupcake base finished on three sides, surmounted by a corkscrew flame.[19] Yet the quiet, understated sensibility speaks to the aesthetic concerns of the conservative, Quaker community on Easton's Point, Newport, where the Goddard-Townsend school had thrived.

According to Moses, the bonnet-top on these case pieces was a "unique Colonial concept," and the resolution of any construction or design dilemmas had to be solved without stylistic precedent. The Newport solution was to define the scroll board with twin raised panels. Other Newport characteristics include removable legs, dovetailed construction of the backboard to the rear stiles, an ogival mid-molding attached to the upper rather than

the lower case, and an attached molding along the inner arch.[20]

The high chest was frequently crafted en suite with a dressing table. The pair was most often found in a bed chamber, although some were located in the parlor. Remarked one chronicler:

Every householder . . . deemed it essential to his convenience or comfort to have an ample chest of drawers in his parlor or sitting room, in which the linen or clothes of the family were always of ready access. . . . It was no sin to rummage them before company![21]

The central line of locks which mark each drawer indicates the high value attached to the goods stored inside. In the nineteenth century, the novelist Nathaniel Hawthorne sentimentally remarked:

. . . the moderns have invented nothing better, as chamber furniture, than these chests of drawers, which stand on four long, slender legs, and near an absolute tower . . . to the ceiling, the whole terminating in a Fantastically carved summit.[22]

The lilting curves of Queen Anne style were eventually adopted by craftsmen in every furniture-making center. However, in Philadelphia, which experienced a period of economic expansion in the 1730s, chairmakers in particular firmly grasped the notion of the reverse curve as a design device. Historian Charles Montgomery once noted: "In the best American Queen Anne style furniture, the form becomes the ornament and is the dominant aspect of the whole."[23] One walnut side-chair dating from the mid 1740s, demonstrates the heights to which the baroque formula rose in the hands of Philadelphia craftsmen (page 28). It combines, in varying degrees, Hogarth's favored line with a plasticity of form: from the crisp outline of the backsplat, to the subtle swirls of the curlicue volutes flanking the crest rail and knee brackets, to the balloon-shaped seat supported by arching, cabriole legs.[24] The line of the "crookt foot" or cabriole leg was derived from the curve of an animal's hind leg. The term stemmed from the Italian word, *capriola,* meaning "to caper or jump" as in the manner of a wild goat.[25]

In this instance, the arched cabriole legs terminate in distinctive trifid feet "with a raised tongue extending up the leg." The trifid foot was a detail of Irish origin, by way of England, which was adapted by Philadelphia craftsmen, and it brings to mind the notion of regional design preference.[26] In Philadelphia there were two traditions of furniture design. The first harkened back to the Quaker sensibility "of the best sort but plain" and was practiced by many native-born craftsmen. The second was generally characterized by more extravagant, richly carved pieces and was considered more the practice of immigrant craftsmen.[27]

The eighteenth-century designer Thomas Sheraton once qualified the purpose of a polescreen or firescreen as "a piece of furniture to shelter the face or legs from the fire."[28] Perhaps more important, however, an elegantly embroidered screen such as the mahogany Boston example, with a carefully worked scene of a shepherdess and her flock, would have served as a showcase for the talents of the embroiderer (page 30).

The degree to which a young woman was educated was proved by the products of her hand, be it a sampler, a painted box or an embroidered stool. The dexterity of her talents reflected upon the entire household for it reinforced expectations of style and organizational skills while it confirmed the ability of her parents to attend to their daughter's schooling. This Boston polescreen is suspended upon a mahogany standard with a removable, spiral-turned finial to allow the user to adjust the height. It is supported by a trio of cabriole legs with acanthus-carved knees ending in typical Massachusetts-style, retracted claw-and-ball feet.

Three-legged tables found particular popularity during the eighteenth century because they provided a sensible foil to the uneven floorboards of colonial homes. A tripod Salem candlestand with a fluted, spiral-carved standard was intended ". . . for the convenience of affording additional light to each part of the room where it would neither be ornamental nor easy to introduce any other kind"

LEFT:
The candlestand was an essential object in the eighteenth-century American home. Because of their frequent use, candlestands needed to be both portable and stable. This Salem, Massachusetts, example offers an elegant solution. The spirally fluted pedestal is supported on a tripod base of cabriole legs with C-scrolled inner knee returns and platformed pad feet. The refined serpentine top successfully complements the liveliness of the base.

ABOVE:
This circa 1755 Boston blockfront kneehole dressing table is constructed of richly figured mahogany. The table integrates the S-curves and verticality of the Queen Anne period with the flat blocking and rococo brasses of the early Chippendale period.

RIGHT:
Another Queen Anne example of Massachusetts blockfront furniture in the Meyer collection is this chest of drawers which is enhanced by tiered brasses, the center column of which is intentionally set a degree higher than its flanking counterparts in order to enhance its verticality. Consequently, the eye is carried inward and upward. The dramatic overhang of the top is visually balanced by the central fan-carved drop pendant of the skirt and the exceptionally tall scroll-cut straight bracket feet.

ABOVE:

Rectangular tea tables were frequently placed on display in eighteenth-century homes as a centerpiece of furniture groupings. This elegant eighteenth-century Newport example reveals distinctive regional construction. The applied rim of the top is rounded on the exterior and has a broad convex inner edge. The top is set within the frame of the skirt into which the slipper-foot cabriole legs grace-fully flow. Also of note in the drawing room is the silver Paul Revere porringer and the circa 1760 Massachusetts mahogany chest of drawers embellished with rounded blocking and original brass side-carrying handles. The oil painting above the chest is signed by Childe Hassam.

(page 32).[29] Lighting devices and candles were a luxury. Many families kept "blind man's holiday" at dusk or when the moon was bright enough to shine through the windows. Yet a pleasant residual effect of the scarcity of light sources was to bring families together in the evening. Recalled one Massachusetts diarist: "When evening came we used to set a candle on the candle stand and pull the stand to the centre of the room so that four people could sit around it and see to work."[30] Certainly the lack of light offered one good reason for the American colonial practice of returning furniture to the border of a room after use because "it would be all too easy to trip over pieces left out."[31] There are numerous renditions in period accounts of accidents that occurred due to a misplaced step during a nighttime grope across a darkened room or stair.

In Boston and other parts of Massachusetts, case furniture with a shaped facade was often fashionable. Sometimes termed "swelled" or "ogee," the surface movement could be formed through a serpentine, bombe or blocked front design.[32] During the third quarter of the eighteenth century, the blockfront form experienced popularity among the wealthy in Boston, Salem, Newport and Connecticut, but was all but rejected by New York, Philadelphia and the Southern states. The large quantities of primary wood needed to craft the stepped facade greatly augmented the cost. In the case of a blockfront "buerow table" made of imported mahogany, the expense of the

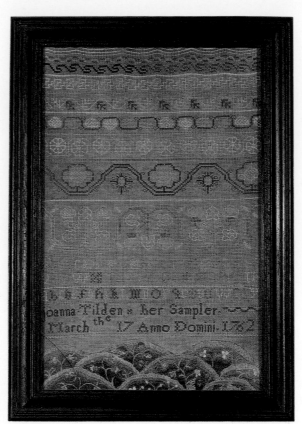

Samplers were the province of young women learning the art of embroidery as both a pastime and a decorative artistic practice. Two wonderful examples from the Meyer collection are illustrated here. Joanna Tilden, the maker of the example on the right, is presumably a young woman born to Jonathan Tilden and Mary Ruck Tilden on 30 November 1744 in Boston, and married to Jonathan Moulton in York, Maine, on June 11, 1765. If she is indeed the artist, she would have completed the sampler at the age of 17.

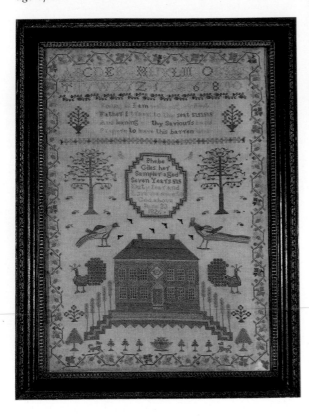

drawer fronts cut from the solid wood would have been great (page 33). In Massachusetts, the blocking was articulated either squared or rounded. In this example, the blocked facade is flat and squared. Boston area designs tended to foster a sense of narrow verticality, accented minimally by the stepped placement of brasses and escutcheons up the raised facade.[33]

The bureau table later was called a kneehole desk because in some designs the top drawer was outfitted with an adjustable writing surface. More generally it was used for the purposes of grooming and would have been found in a bed chamber. Inventories suggest that the drawers would have contained the various implements of the toilet, while the central recessed panel marked by a "prospect door" opened into a space that was used by some owners to secret a wigstand.[34] A 1763 inventory of "Coll. Robert Oliver . . . of Dorchester," included a bureau table in his "Marble Chamber" which was also furnished with a bedstead, a chest of drawers, and "6 leather bottomed chairs." Meanwhile the 1786 inventory of John Cadwalader included two bureau tables, the first, in the "Front room 3rd story," was of mahogany, while the second was positioned in the corresponding "Front chamber" of the second floor.[35]

A mahogany blocked chest of drawers dating from *circa* 1770 also features some of the stylistic nuances characteristic of Massachusetts pieces (page 35). The top overhangs the case on all four sides and is patterned to the shape of the drawers below. The case is raised on high bracket feet while the apron is marked by a single drop shell ornament. The blocking is squared, flat and narrow and is emphasized by the use of large shaped brasses. ★

The Jonathan Jackson Queen Anne Walnut Blockfront Secretary Bookcase

On Sunday, October 28, 1781, the Honorable Jonathan Jackson of Newburyport, Massachusetts, wrote to his brother-in-law, concerning news of the War's end:

> Our citizens (than whom none more loyally partake in everything tending to the welfare of America) began in half-an-hour after the news came into the Town on Friday (and that was between two and three,) & held it incessantly till last evening & some of them rather encroached upon the ritual decency of that—in short, if bells & cannon shouts & bonfires demonstrate joy we have had our share.[1]

Jackson had been a member of the Provincial Congress during the Revolution. He later became a member of Congress, a State Senator, Supervisor of Excises, Treasurer of the Commonwealth of Massachusetts, and a Fellow and Treasurer of Harvard University. He was also the original owner of this blockfront secretary, which was subsequently passed down through four generations of the Jackson family.[2] No doubt such an elegant piece, decorated with classical motifs, attested to the sophisticated taste and intellectual pedigree of its owner when it was crafted in the 1740s. After all, this was a cool character who at age 29 extended a casual invitation to a friend on the occasion of his marriage to the 17-year-old Hannah Tracey: "You may travel that road that day you know—"Verbum sapienti Sat est"—should I have omitted anything necessary to the procuring of a [marriage] License, you will dispatch the Messenger back on Saturday as early as may be."[3]

Furniture historian Alan Miller has extensively studied a group of similar case pieces from Boston. He surmised that the inspiration for the group came from a Boston cabinet shop

that was either supervised by a British-trained designer or by a native-born craftsman who had visited England in the 1720s or 1730s, long enough to absorb British fashions. If so, this craftsman had visited England just as British designers were adopting the "new classical interpretations, or Roman 'gusto'." Many of the new patterns were derived from the designs of the Italian architect, Andrea Palladio (1508–80), who had looked to sources in Roman antiquity for his own buildings. Palladio's designs had been introduced to England in the writings of Inigo Jones and Colen Campbell. And, the contagious nature of furniture fashions being what they were, the aesthetic metamorphosis experienced by British designers was observed by an unidentified American craftsman whose technique was then absorbed by a rival Boston shop that created the blockfront secretary used by Jonathan Jackson.[4]

Most colonial cabinetry shops operated on a piecework system whereby the collaborative efforts of several talented specialists—a designer, a joiner, a turner, a gilder or japanner and a carver—were pooled to create exceptional case pieces. In this instance, the molded pediment centered by a gilded flaming urn finial, the beveled mirror panels on the arched doors, each bordered by Corinthian pilasters, the stepped desk interior with a concave blocked prospect door, the line inlay and interior arches decorated with dual inlaid lunettes, reveal the talents of many expert hands.

This secretary was purchased by Jess Pavey for the Meyers and was included in the Parke-Bernet Galleries, Inc., sale of The Collection of Maurice Rubin on October 9, 1954.

1. Elizabeth Cabot Putnam and James Jackson, eds., *The Honorable Jonathan Jackson and Hannah (Tracy) Jackson: Their Ancestors and Descendants* (Boston: T. R. Marrin and Son, 1907), p. v.
2. *Important XVIII Century American Furniture From the Collection of Maurice Rubin, Brookline, Mass.,* October 9, 1954 (New York: Parke-Bernet Galleries, Inc.), lot 174.
3. Putnam and Jackson, *Jackson,* p. vi.
4. Alan Miller, "Roman Gusto in New England: An Eighteenth-Century Boston Furniture Designer and His Shop," in *American Furniture 1993,* ed. Luke Beckerdite (Hanover, N.H.: University Press of New England for the Chipstone Foundation, 1993), p. 161.

Chippendale Furniture

This exquisite Chippendale mahogany wing armchair made in Boston, circa 1755, features elegantly curved front cabriole legs ending in naturalistically carved feet comprising four bird's talons clutching a ball.

The term rococo comes from the French word, 'rocaille', after the elaborate rockworks and "artificial caves or grottos, themselves evocative of aquatic fantasies, in the seventeenth-century pleasure gardens of the [French] aristocracy." In the latter part of the eighteenth century, English furniture patterns began to feature rococo elements such as foliate carving, cartouches, shells and other grotto-themed ornamentation. The man whose name has since become synonymous with the designs of this period is Thomas Chippendale. In 1754 Chippendale published *The Gentleman & Cabinet-Maker's Director* in London. The premise of the book was to provide a reference for the latest English furniture patterns, in addition to setting forth a number of Chippendale's own designs. In America, as in England, the *Director* found interested audiences. Chippendale was not the only merchant-craftsman to promote style through a pattern book. Other publications included Matthias Locke's *New Book of Ornaments* (1752), Thomas Johnson's *New Book of Ornaments* (1760), Ince and Mayhew's *Universal System of Household Furniture* (1760), and Robert Manwaring's *Cabinet and Chair-Maker's Real Friend and Companion* (1765). However, because of clever marketing, the Chippendale name became inextricably linked to late eighteenth-century American rococo furniture designs.[1]

Furniture and architecture share a number of basic tenets. Differences of scale aside, in both cases, the vocabulary of decorative detail is built around similar issues of balance between vertical and horizontal proportions and a concern for both interior and exterior space. Because furniture is a smaller medium, it is more adaptable to the winds of stylistic change.[2] What is now identified as Chippendale style in American decoration really involved a synthesis of existing English interpretations of neo-

The top of this elegant Philadelphia piecrust-top tea table is constructed of a single thirty-three-inch board of golden-brown-colored mahogany. Helen Comstock has noted that the serpentine curve of the alternately scalloped and plain edge of the top was a form developed by English silversmiths for salvers in the 1730s. The table is raised on a gracefully turned pillar with a compressed ball above a ribbon- and flowerhead-carved ring. The tripod base is decorated with classic Philadelphia acanthus-leaf carving and claw-and-ball feet. Interestingly, it has been said that the venerable firm of Israel Sack, Inc., acquired and sold this magnificent tea table on three separate occasions.

The birdcage support is characteristic of Philadelphia construction and is rarely found on New England tilt-top tables. It is constructed of two square boards connected by lathe-turned baluster supports. At one end is a spring catch which fastens into the brass lock, holding the top in a sturdy horizontal position.

Palladian techniques and designs with an applique of rococo trimmings. The fashion emphasized carved ornamentation, the use of figured surfaces, the interplay between light and dark contrasts and a new appreciation for shining and reflective surfaces. The extended title of the Chippendale book, which had two subsequent editions in 1755 and 1762, included the following tag line: "Being a large collection of the most Elegant and Useful Designs of Household Furniture in the Gothic, Chinese and Modern Taste."[3] Chippendale postulated that upon a basic comprehension of classical design theory, a craftsman could update his furniture style using an overlay of French patterns, modern Gothic or medieval designs, or modified Chinese or Far Eastern motifs.

Just after the mid-century mark, Philadelphia was climbing to the head of colonial influence, power and wealth as an urban center. One writer had termed it the "Athens of America," while William M. Hornor, Jr., who chronicled the city's decorative arts in his 1935 *Blue Book: Philadelphia Furniture*, asserted: "The Golden Age of Philadelphia furniture-making occurred during the brilliant Chippendale period in America—roughly speaking from 1745–1789."[4] Located where the Schuylkill and Delaware Rivers meet, Philadelphia maintained an ideal position for shipping, unsurpassed until the late 1790s when New York superseded it in foreign imports. In addi-

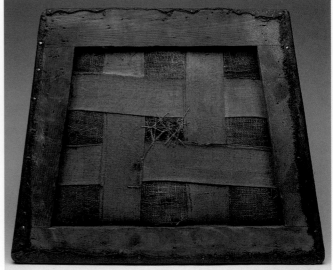

*Elegant restraint and simplicity is evident
in the design of this circa 1760 leather-
upholstered walnut open armchair from
Philadelphia. The slip-seat is covered
with the original leather upholstery, typically stuffed with marsh grass and horsehair. The through-tenons from the side
rails into the back legs are characteristic
of Philadelphia construction as are the
curves of the scrolled strapwork of the
baluster-shaped pierced splat. The
armchair was once owned by the pioneer
collector of American furniture,
Dwight Blaney, and was displayed in
Boston, Massachusetts, at the 1911
Copley Society Exhibition.*

tion, a new network of land routes to the West strength-
ened domestic trade possibilities. Jacques Brissot de
Warville remarked in 1788 of the city's growth:

*Philadelphia may be considered the metropolis of the
United States. It is certainly the most beautiful and
best-built city in the nation, and also the wealthiest,
though not the most ostentatious. Here you find more
well-educated men, more knowledge of politics and
literature, more political and learned societies than
anywhere else in the United States.[5]*

Boston had waned in prominence, and although New
York was only second in size to Philadelphia, one-third of
its residents had been loyal to the Crown and vacated
the city at the end of the War for Independence in 1783.
Meanwhile, Philadelphia's port was booming, and the
immigrant craftsmen who filtered into the economic
capital of the colonies, found a monied and culturally
aware citizenry awaiting the best and latest that their
skills could produce.

Connecticut's representative to the Continental
Congress, Silas Deane, once remarked that in Philadelphia,
"hospitality itself resides." The eminently popular tea
ceremony provided excellent opportunity for such gra-
ciousness. The ritual of tea-drinking had entered the
American social scene in the 1730s, and by mid century,
an entire code of etiquette had been developed around
the drink. It was not unusual to serve tea twice a day.

continued on page 50

The Edmund Townsend Block- and Shell-Carved Mahogany Kneehole Desk

This Newport, Rhode Island, blockfront "bureau table" was purchased for the Meyers during the 1950 auction of the Collection of Mr. and Mrs. Norvin H. Green at Parke-Bernet Galleries, Inc., by their advisor and Birmingham-based dealer, Jess Pavey. Pavey agreed with the language of the auction catalogue which had termed it a "superlative desk . . . [which has] . . . remained continuously in untouched condition, without even surface treatment, and therefore remains original in all respects, including color and patination."[1] And, when the gavel fell at the sale, Pavey recalled the auctioneer, Hiram Parke, doing something absolutely unheard of in an auction-room setting. Parke stepped away from the podium, walked over to the dealer and congratulated him for having acquired the "finest piece I have ever had the privilege of selling at auction." Indeed, in the hands of Newport's Townsend and Goddard craftsmen, American blockfront design reached its apex, and the mahogany kneehole desk purchased at the Green sale that day proved to be an exceptional case in point.

For years, speculation has abounded as to the origins of the blockfront form. In 1941, one collector of Americana, Maxim Karolik, posited:

Where did the blockfront design originate? God knows. Probably stolen from somewhere. We all know that the Americans 'stole' from the English; the English from the French; the French from the Italians; the Italians from the Greeks; and all of them together 'stole' a great deal from the Ancient East, especially from China . . . This [blockfront] design, in its richness and beauty, has a majestic simplicity, the secret of which was well known to the ancient Chinese.[2]

Certainly no English prototype for the blockfront design has been identified. Although in 1762, Chippendale published a blockfront design in the third edition of his furniture guide, its publication postdated John Townsend's earliest Newport design by almost six years.[3]

Furniture historian John Kirk has written of the marked similarity between American blockfront designs and that of contemporary German and French pieces.[4] Another writer, Michael Moses agreed that French ties to the form were valid because a number of Newport furniture designs dating from the 1750s display a distinctive French flavor. Furthermore, quite a few French families were living in Newport by the early eighteenth century and many of them had "commercial dealings" with the Townsends.[5]

From the 1740s to the 1790s, blockfront designs met enormous popularity on American soil, particularly in Rhode Island and Massachusetts. Some historians have speculated that American blockfront design was pioneered in Boston, but perfected in Newport. The existence of a stagecoach line between the two towns by 1736, coupled

with an ever-heightening degree of coastal shipping, certainly assured that "sufficient exchanges were made between the two cities." This guaranteed "that the latest design feature developed in one location would be rapidly communicated, either by word or example, to the other."[6]

Regardless of its origins, the realization of the four-shell, blockfront facade on the Meyers' "bureau table" or kneehole desk is masterful. Its crisply rendered design has been attributed to the hand of Edmund Townsend, the second son of Job Townsend, the founding father of the Townsend dynasty. Surprisingly little is known of the life of Edmund Townsend who was born in Newport in 1736. Much of what has been established as to his craft practices is based upon the sole labeled example of his work—a four-shell, kneehole desk in the Karolik collection at the Boston Museum of Fine Arts. A three-shell kneehole desk which dates to the late 1760s and had a history in the Deshon family of New London, Connecticut, bears Townsend's signature on the case.

The execution of the Boston Museum's labeled kneehole desk which dates to roughly 1775, and the Meyer example which dates to *circa* 1780, is virtually identical. Both desks are elegantly defined by the counterpulsing rhythms of the blockfront vertical panels and the horizontality of the drawers. In the catalogue to the Boston Museum's Karolik collection, Edwin J. Hipkiss remarked of Townsend's design: "His kneehole bureau has a graceful lightness; it has not the robustness, the sturdiness of the other known kneehole bureaus." Hipkiss further described: "The shells, the concave door which is correspondingly convex at the back, and the ogee feet with the 'curlicue' coming down, all show the delicate touch of a master hand."[7]

Other shared details include the thumb-molded tops and the base moldings in which the bracket feet meet in the front. In each instance, the ogee bracket feet have C-scroll marginal carving ending in sculpted volutes. Both desks have bead molding surrounding each drawer which is attached to the case. Similarly, the convex shells which mark the outer vertical line of the blocked facade are defined by eleven concave lobes while the rosette patterns of the flanking shells are fashioned of seven petals defined by stop-fluted stems. However, in the Boston Museum example, the first and last lobes are connected by a bar across the base while in the Meyer piece this bar is absent.[8]

When Edmund Townsend died in 1811, his estate was valued at $1,000. The estate inventory included "one dining room table with claw feet; one mahogany breakfast table with wings and fluted legs; six leather-bottom chairs; [and] one mahogany desk." The varied contents of his will reveal the diverse nature of his craft, despite the paucity of extant labeled pieces today. Moreover, his obituary in the *Newport Mercury* of November 30th reported, "For nearly thirty-nine years he was Town Treasurer of this Town: the duties of which office were always fulfilled with honor to himself, and to the advantage of the Town."[9] Such is the peculiar nature of fame, that in his time, the gifted craftsman Edmund Townsend was lauded for his civic responsibility rather than for his exceptional artistry.

1. *The Notable American Collection of Mr. and Mrs. Norvin H. Green,* November 29, 30, and December 1, 2 (New York: Parke-Bernet, 1950), lot 663.
2. Edwin J. Hipkiss, *Eighteenth-Century American Arts: The M. and M. Karolik Collection* (Cambridge: Harvard University Press for the Museum of Fine Arts, Boston, 1941), p. 352.
3. Michael Moses, *Master Craftsmen of Newport: The Townsends and Goddards* (Tenafly, N.J.: By the author, 1984), p. 4.
4. John T. Kirk, *American Furniture and the British Tradition to 1830* (New York: Alfred A. Knopf, 1982), pp. 125–128.
5. Moses, p. 5.
6. Moses, p. 6.
7. Hipkiss, p. 355.
8. Moses, pp. 268–269.
9. Hipkiss, p. 68.

American silversmiths continued to manufacture the English porringer form long after its popularity waned in England. Porringers, most often seen with engraved initials, were found in almost every New England home, a proliferation which has led scholars to conclude that the porringer was a traditional eighteenth-century gift. This initialed example was made and stamped by Paul Revere, the Boston silversmith who was immortalized as a patriot by Henry Wadsworth Longfellow's poem, The Midnight Ride of Paul Revere, *which took place on April 19, 1775.*

One visitor to 1781 Boston, Baron Cromot du Bourg, noted that the Americans drank "a great deal of tea in the morning [and] about five o'clock they take more tea, some wine, Madeira [and] punch."[6] Despite the cost of the precious tea leaves, however, one contemporary cynic observed: "Tea parties, were invented by Avarice, in order to see company cheap."[7]

A mahogany table with a "scollop'd edge" was a form that found great popularity in Philadelphia during the advent of rococo designs (page 42). The scalloped or piecrust-edged top was cut from a single wide board of purple-hued mahogany and mounted upon a birdcage mechanism to allow the table to tilt and turn. John Fannig Watson, a chronicler of colonial life, wrote in 1828: "They had mahogany tea boards and round tea tables, which, being turned on an axle underneath the centre, stood upright, like an expanded fan or palm leaf, in the corner."[8] Indeed, the ingenious nature of the birdcage mechanism satisfied the colonial American preference that unused furniture be placed upon the periphery of a room.

The taste for vigorously carved furniture forms coincided with a heightened influx of mahogany from the West Indies. Mahogany was an ideal wood for rococo fashions because it was dense, strong, and could be easily carved. As with most furniture, scalloped-edge tea tables were usually crafted as composite pieces. There were carvers and turners who specialized in "pillars and claws," and other craftsmen who advertised the manufacture of tops "for tea tables of French mahogany."[9] Similarly, a table made by a native-born craftsman such as William Savery might have been ornamented by Bernard and Jugiez, the duo of London carvers, who relocated to Philadelphia around 1762.

As explained by Benjamin Franklin in a letter to his wife, the breakfast table was protected by a cloth or napkin during use. His letter from London dated February 19, 1758, instructed: "They are to be spread on the Tea Table, for nobody breakfasts here [London] on the naked Table but on the Cloth set a large Tea Board with Cups." The molded edge of the piecrust design often echoed in the borders of the silver salvers and tea trays used on the table's surface. The 1793 estate inventory of an elderly

Philadelphia matron, Deborah Morris, revealed the extent of her silver tea service.

1 coffee pot, 1 tea pot

1 slop bowl, 1 sugar bowl

1 cream jug, 11 tea spoons

1 sugar tongs, 1 strainer spoon

1 tea spoon tray[10]

The design of a claw-and-ball foot was derived from a centuries-old Chinese motif of a dragon talon clutching a pearl. Although it was fervently adapted by American craftsmen, Chippendale's *Director* used the motif in only one illustration, that of a tea caddy. Hornor wrote: "Ball-and-claw feet are always at their best on a tripod table, for the ankle can be sufficiently slender without weakening the support and the claw extends in such an angle that it stretches over the ball, actually grasping it."[11] Regard the Meyer example, for the attenuation of the jointed claw is superb. Also noteworthy are the intricately carved sprays of Mediterranean acanthus leaves which inch down the front of the legs. One critic remarked that a master carver did not "muscularize nor fibrate too much, nor yet to leave the foliage bare nor the figures like a stuffed sack."[12] In this instance, the carver was well able to adjust the proportions of his scheme to the dimensions of the piece.

As for the easy chair, its overall outline evolved slowly through the century. The claw-and-ball feet on the front legs of a *circa* 1755 walnut Massachusetts easy chair demonstrate the subtlety of the change (page 41). The chair retains the turned stretchers, high rectilinear back and the upright, outward-scrolling arms of the previously pictured Queen Anne example (page 25). A shift occurs in the use of claw-and-ball feet to replace the pad feet of the earlier form and in a more pronounced arch in the crest rail. Unlike many of their New England counterparts, Massachusetts craftsmen were slow to cease the use of stretchers for additional structural support, as demonstrated by a *circa* 1765 New York easy chair which lacks stretchers, yet was crafted almost contemporaneously (page 59). The overall stature of the chair demonstrates the broader proportions of New York furniture during the Chippendale period compared with that of other design centers.

Chinese export porcelain enjoyed great popularity in American homes. Among the luxury items exported for the American market was this beautiful porcelain punchbowl, decorated on the exterior with birds and chinoiserie motifs. The interior features an elaborate border of butterflies, flowers and cornucopias.

As mentioned in the discussion of Queen Anne side chairs, the Philadelphia cabinetmaking community was comprised of native-born craftsmen, who tended to create "plainer" fashions which appealed to the Quaker sensibility of the city, and London-trained immigrant craftsmen, who promoted more costly, ornate European-inspired designs. However, those who patronized these artisans were not divided along ideological lines. A number of existing account and receipt books indicate that furniture of both sorts was purchased by the same buyers. For example, the wealthy John Cadwalader patronized the London-trained Thomas Affleck for the lavish furnishings of his public rooms, while he tapped the talents of the locally-trained artisan, William Savery, for more modest fashions to adorn his lesser rooms.[13]

A carved walnut armchair dating to *circa* 1760 demonstrates the sort of tempered rococo design that was peculiar to Philadelphia (page 45). The rectangular back, the pierced baluster splat, the drop-in trapezoidal seat within a molded framework and the claw-and-ball feet are basic Chippendale motifs. Elements such as the molded arms and arm supports, the cabriole front legs, flared stump back legs and the applied scallop-shell ornament centered along the crest rail recall aspects of Queen Anne design. The chair retains its original black leather seat which must have struck a chord with a later owner and notable Massachusetts antiquarian, Dwight Blaney (1865–1944).

Blaney was a member of the Walpole Society, a group which took its name from the eighteenth-century collector Horace Walpole because "he was the discoverer of English arts and crafts at a time when polite society could appreciate only the foreign." Similarly, early members of the Walpole Society sought to direct "public attention to the merit of American work in an era when the foreign was the thing."[14] Blaney claimed that "life began to carry on" only after he had become a member of the group. One of his compatriots, Henry Kent, said of Blaney:

> He was full of surprises and delights. He was possessed of real knowledge of our early crafts and craftsmen . . . and, being a craftsman himself, he had a fellow feeling for other workmen; but he was possessed, also, of what was even more important, the spirit of the times when such works of craftsmanship as those he collected were made and used.[15]

LEFT:
Pembroke tables, also known as breakfast tables, were in fact multi-purpose, often ranging in use as a desk, workstand, tea table, or dining table. The stylistic characteristics of this rare fully-developed Philadelphia pembroke table are transitional between the Chippendale and the early Federal styles. The table is wonderfully animated by pierced corner brackets and highly arched stretchers.

ABOVE:
Charles Willson Peale is known in particular for his portraits of heroes of the American Revolution. In this beautifully executed painting, signed and dated 1789, Peale depicts Major John Berrien (1760–1815). After the war's end, Major Berrien was decorated with the "Eagle of Cincinnati" by George Washington. The large book in his right hand reads, Lex/Parliamen, *the legal nature of which refers to his profession as a lawyer following the war. The portrait is encased in a rare and exquisitely carved eighteenth-century giltwood frame.*

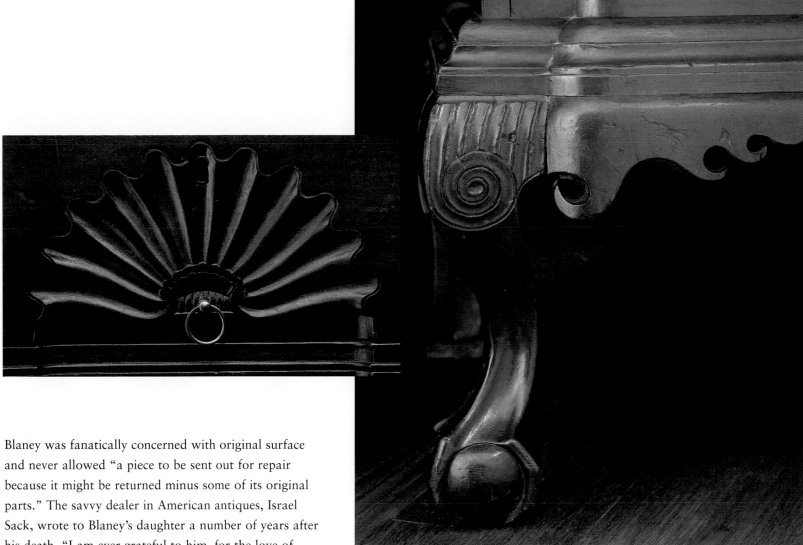

Blaney was fanatically concerned with original surface and never allowed "a piece to be sent out for repair because it might be returned minus some of its original parts." The savvy dealer in American antiques, Israel Sack, wrote to Blaney's daughter a number of years after his death, "I am ever grateful to him, for the love of Americana he imbued in me."[16]

Chippendale updated his *Director* twice following the initial publication in 1754. Both the first and the 1762 editions included a table with four stationary legs, two leaves and two swing brackets under the heading "Breakfast Table." By the time Thomas Sheraton published his design book in 1793 he had incorporated the popular term "Pembroke Table" to describe the form which he claimed came from "the lady who first gave orders for one of them, and who probably gave the first idea of such a table to the workmen." Sheraton further described: "The use of this piece is for a gentleman or lady to breakfast on."[17] Period accounts indicate they were also used for occasional refreshment, solitary dining, sewing, writing, and cardplay.

A Philadelphia mahogany Pembroke table is derived from Plate LIII of the 1754 edition of Chippendale's *Director* (page 52). It is comprised of two shaped leaves, four fixed Marlborough legs joined by crossed stretchers

continued on page 58

This circa 1780 Connecticut cherrywood interpretation of the Newport block-and-shell form shows the influence of "high-style" furniture from urban centers such as Newport and Boston. The block-and-shell motif on this chest differs from its more urban counterpart. The cabinet-maker incorporated several details not found on Newport blockfront chests of drawers such as the cabriole leg with claw-and-ball foot and the elaborate series of moldings which join the body of the case with the feet. The carved shells, the centers of which are ornamented with splayed stop-fluted lobes, and the stylized carving of the claw-and-ball feet bear a close resemblance to those on pieces documented to Benjamin Burnham of Colchester, Connecticut.

A Selection of Chairs in the Meyer Collection

Chairbacks are a major indicator of style. This survey of
chairbacks in the Meyer collection places these chairs
in a more or less chronological order, beginning at the
upper left. However, it is important to consider that styles
not only overlap, but continue well beyond the linear
time boundaries which have been established by history.
Thus, when dating American chairs, one must always
look to the latest feature in chair backs. These pages encompass the Queen Anne, Chippendale and Federal styles.

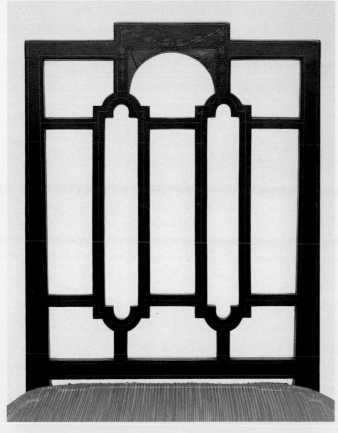

This circa 1785 *mahogany card table is one of a small group of related tables from Rhode Island with stop-fluted square legs. The earliest reference to American stop-fluted furniture occurs in the bills of Christopher Champlin where he makes note of a maple bedstead ordered from the Goddard-Townsend craftsmen in 1787.*

and an apron marked by a single drawer. The illustration in the *Director* featured a table with horizontal, flat pierced stretchers. By contrast, the Philadelphia example used solid stretchers, arched and lapped together at the center and crowned by a pierced vase. In both cases, when the leaves were extended, they were supported by swing rails or "flys." The crossed stretchers allowed for comfortable foot and leg room while the "graceful dome[d] shape" of the Philadelphia example intensified the sculptural nature of the form.[18] Furthermore, the Chinese-inspired fretwork brackets served as a visual segue between the horizontal thrust of the table top and the vertical impulse of the legs.

In many ways, Connecticut served as a melting pot for domestic style sources stemming from Boston, Newport, New York and Philadelphia.[19] A blockfront chest, possibly from Colchester, serves as a case in point as to why Connecticut's particular physical and economic position resulted in a number of stylistically idiosyncratic furniture designs (page 54). The three-drawer case piece features three blockfront panels surmounted by carved shells, and is a clear derivative of Newport's Goddard-Townsend tradition. Yet, because it is crafted of cherrywood rather than mahogany, and because it is raised on high cabriole front legs, and because it has oddly rendered volutes on the knee brackets, it leaves no doubt as to its vernacular roots. A "metropolitan" designer might have strived for a more overall unity of parts, but the visual astonishment of these simple details is what makes the chest such a fascinating piece.[20]

Since its establishment, Connecticut's economy experienced periods of acute expansion and retraction. Norwich, New London and Colchester were small-fry import communities compared to the major urban centers such as Boston, Philadelphia and Newport. However, during the Revolutionary War, a number of Connecticut merchants made large profits supplying the troops and subsequently had money to spend on their homes and furnishings following the war. Furniture historian, Robert Trent asserted that the aspirations of these patrons had direct repercussions on local furniture designs. Cabinetmakers were deluged with requests for case pieces, often by members of the same extended family. The pressure to produce many variations of the same pieces "undoubtedly explains the free combination of Boston, Newport and Philadelphia compositional strategies that characterized much eastern Connecticut work."[21]

Thus, rather than the product of a craftsman's naivete concerning a Newport form, the peculiarities in the design of the chest resulted from a temporary swell in patronage. Connecticut was located in the path of many stylistic currents and cabinetmakers "synthesized these influences as best they could." According to Trent, the result was a decorative vocabulary which looked to Newport for the blockfront facade surmounted by shells and for the use of cove molding under the top and along the base. Similarly, the front cabriole legs raised on claw-and-ball feet were derivative of Philadelphia style as was the incised scroll carving on the knees which "must be seen as an attempt to supply rococo scrollwork . . . where the training to execute it was wanting." The odd combination of the cabriole leg with a bracket rear foot is "difficult to explain," however it confirms that the chest of drawers was placed at a wallside location and that the craftsman had seen no need to ornament barely visible detail.[22]

A young John Adams once criticized those who "waste their bloom of life at the card or billiard table among rakes and fools."[23] Despite his words, by the 1770s, the playing of cards or dice in America had become a firmly entrenched and accepted social activity. The rise in popularity of games such as whist, poker, cribbage and loo in both England and America spawned an outgrowth of furniture designed specifically for the purposes of such play, frequently ordered in pairs by wealthy colonial citizens. John Cadwalader owned two sets of card tables including "2 Commode card tables" obtained from Thomas Affleck.[24] Meanwhile, Jerathmiel Pierce of Salem, kept "2 mahogany Card Tables" in his drawing room, while Aaron Burr of New York kept two in the "Blue or drawing rooms" of his townhouse.[25]

Newport tables supported by straight Marlborough legs with stop-fluted carving have as yet been traced only to the hand of master craftsman John Townsend. The will of his cousin, Edmund Townsend, indicated that he too made stop-fluted furniture, although no labeled or signed examples have surfaced.[26] In any case, the airy fashion of the stop-fluted straight legs paired with pierced brackets that support a Newport card table were inspired by

This easy chair, made circa 1765, *is characterized by substantial proportions typical of New York. Sturdy cabriole legs, tenoned into the seat rail, prevent the need of stretchers. Note the squared claw-and-ball feet which are discussed on pages 66–67.*

Chinese Chippendale motifs (page 58). The table dates to the 1780s and features a rectangular top with a serpentine front. Formed from the solid, the serpentine frame is complemented by the chip-carved edge on the folding leaf and similarly chip-carved apron border. Predictably, the folding top permitted the table flexible usage as a console or pier table. Or, as was described by George Washington in 1759, "a neat Make Card Table—wch may serve for a dress^g one."[27]

The chamber table or dressing table customarily served as a companion piece to a high chest of drawers in a colonial bed chamber. Hornor noted that every high chest had its "table to suit," and that wealthier clients often had sets of chamber chairs which worked en suite with the "embellishments and corner finish."[28] Because the dressing table was intended for the purposes of grooming, a large looking glass usually hung above it on the wall or a small, standing mirror was placed upon the surface. A descriptive 1779 inventory of Philadelphian Benjamin Chew's best chamber included:

One mahogany Table with Drawers
One Small Chamber Clock   *On it*
One looking Glass   *Over it.*
One Box with a wig   *Under it.*[29]

Period accounts and prints reveal that it was rare for the surface of a dressing table to remain uncovered. The top was usually kept covered with a cloth or "toilet" of "damask, diaper, calico, or dimity, trimmed with fringe," while a wide array of "paints, pomatums, essences, patches, pincushion, powder box and brushes," was inevitably scattered upon its surface.[30]

Most designs such as this *circa* 1770 Philadelphia model had four drawers. The bureau table illustrated in the past chapter was a related form "more akin visually" to a chest of drawers.[31] Philadelphia craftsman David Evans noted in his account books "a Walnut Beaurou table with Cullum Corners" made for a client in 1785 and a second "beaurow Table cullum Corners" which he made for a baker.[32] These descriptions suit a *circa* 1770 walnut model with engaged fluted corner columns leading to squared cabriole legs (left). Like the block-front bureau table, a chamber table often doubled as a writing surface. However, as the Chippendale carvers began to ornament

LEFT:
The eighteenth-century bedchamber was as much a private place as it was a public place. As Elisabeth Donaghy Garrett has noted in her book, At Home; The American Family 1750–1870, *frequency of childbirth and the following period of extended recovery confined the new mother to the bedchamber where she was visited by friends and family. Consequently, the bedchamber was furnished with useful objects for public display. This walnut dressing table, probably made en suite with a chest of drawers, was most certainly an object of pride to its owner. Refined elegance exudes from the rococo carving and pierced brasses of this brilliant example of the high Chippendale style in Philadelphia.*

ABOVE:
Because dressing tables were often placed against the wall, it is rare for a patron to have ordered one with carving on all four legs. Such a request would have certainly increased the purchase price of the table.

ABOVE:

The recessed shell of the central drawer is carved with stop-fluted lobes. Punchwork decorates the background which is repeated in the knee carving. Dense leafage flows outward flanking the shell.

RIGHT:

A front leg detail of the Chippendale Philadelphia dressing table

the center drawer with more elaborate rococo motifs and artfully extend the apron past the drawer line, its convenience as a writing surface was diminished. The popularity of matched sets of case furniture for the bedroom continued until century's close when it became de rigeur for newly built homes to include closets in the floor plan.

An elegant, great open armchair with a fascinating family history in Philadelphia is derived from Plate XIX of Chippendale's 1762 *Director* (page 64). Chippendale termed the design a "French Chair." It featured an upholstered back and Marlborough legs and was more commonly made for clients in London than in Philadelphia.[33] This rare example was noted in Hornor's *Blue Book* to have descended in the family of Thomas Wharton, the first governor of Pennsylvania.[34] However a small plaque on the back of the mahogany chair reveals that the chair was in fact owned by his brother, Joseph. It bears the inscription: "Chair of my Great-Grandfather Joseph Wharton," and it is signed "Chas. W. Wharton."

According to a nineteenth-century family biographer, Anne Hollingsworth Wharton, Joseph Wharton, Sr., "was known by his contemporaries as 'Duke Wharton', which sobriquet he received in consequence of the dignity and stateliness of his bearing." Wharton owned a country estate on the outskirts of Philadelphia known as Walnut Grove. In a letter to his wife dated September 1774, Silas Deane wrote:

We dined yesterday with Mr. Wharton, a plain hospitable Quaker family of great connections in this City and on this Continent as well as in Europe; but I think has as much of the Serpent as the Dove in his composition. He treated us with the utmost politeness, and carried us in his coach after dinner to his country seat, about ten miles south of the City, to view the country which is fine and rich almost beyond comparison.[35]

Almost a century later, on June 1, 1862, the Philadelphia *Sunday Dispatch* reported on the destruction of Walnut Grove.

The Old Wharton House Coming Down—One of the few surviving relics of the Revolutionary days. . . . In colonial times it was the country seat of the Whartons, an old wealthy aristocratic family of the city. Hither they remained in the warm season from their city residence to spend their time luxuriously amid the shady groves and fragrant gardens of the Southwark Seat. . . . The Delaware flowed pleasantly along in front of the wide grounds belonging to the mansion, and the fortunate Whartons had a genuine earthly elysium.[36]

Hornor identified the chair's maker as Thomas Affleck because "It is Not Difficult to Point Him Out as the Maker When This Chair is Compared with Other Known Products of the Affleck Shop."[37] Additional Affleck attributions have been attached to other pieces which descended in the Wharton family, and the chairmaker is said to have made a set of similar French Chairs for John Penn, the grandson of William, between 1763–66 and later in 1792–3. The Penn attribution was based upon accounts in Affleck's account books which have since disappeared. Interestingly, although the Library Company of Philadelphia owned an edition of the *Director* in 1770,

continued on page 69

Chippendale Furniture

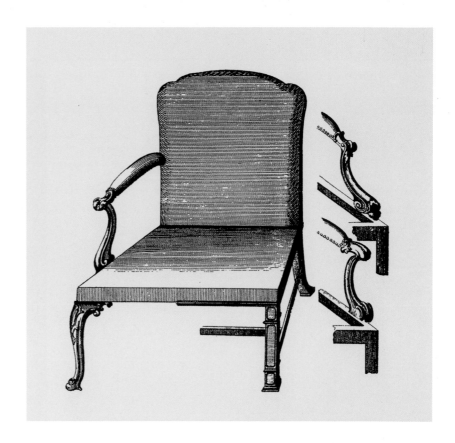

T. Chippendale invᵗ et del.

A Chippendale Carved Mahogany Open Armchair, *Philadelphia,* circa 1770

This well-documented chair made for Joseph Wharton of Philadelphia was directly inspired by a plate in Thomas Chippendale's The Gentleman and Cabinet-Maker's Director, *London, 1762.*

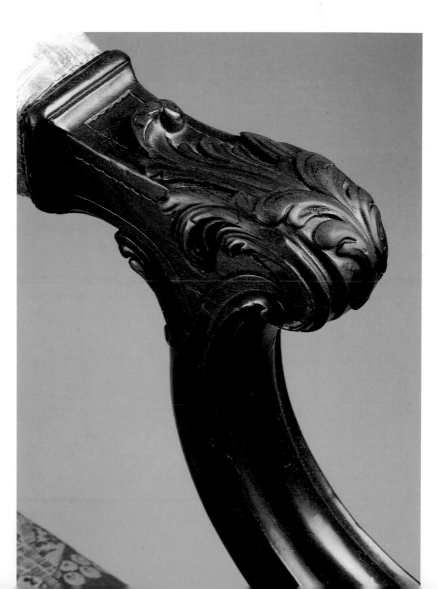

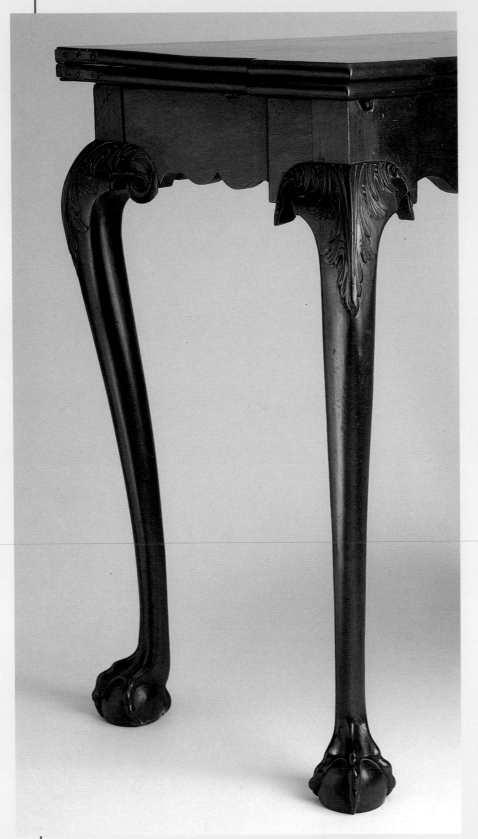

Regional Differences in Chippendale Tables and Chairs in the Meyer Collection

The claw-and-ball foot is one of the earmarks of the Chippendale style. Its widespread use on furniture from each colonial style center has led to its virtual synonymity with the Chippendale style. Interestingly, the only appearance of the claw-and-ball foot in Thomas Chippendale's *Director* is found on a tea caddy. American craftsmen, however, showed a predilection for the claw-and-ball foot and applied it to a variety of furniture forms, as its sculptural mass was well-suited to the fashionable weightiness and rococo carving of the era. The basic claw-and-ball foot flows from a cabriole leg into four carved claws grasping a ball. The delineation of the claws, web, and the shape of the ball, however, vary from region to region.

A side view of a Boston card table

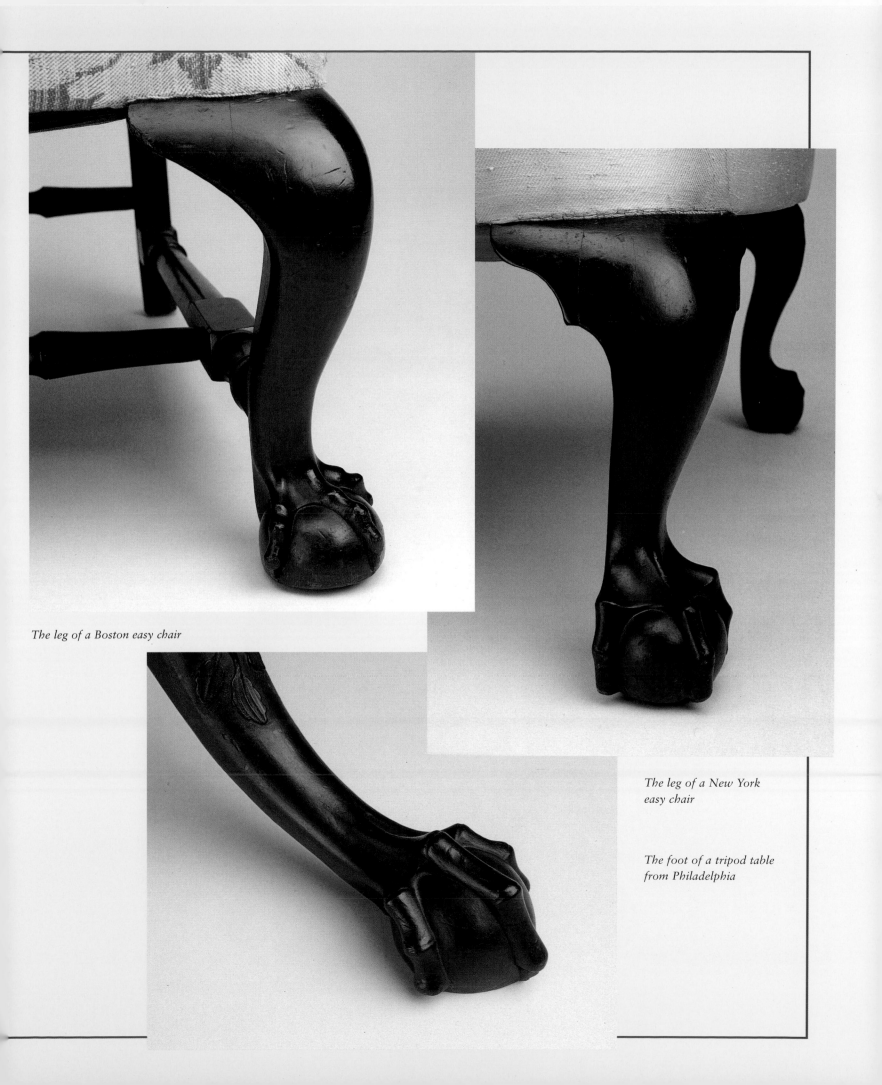

The leg of a Boston easy chair

The leg of a New York easy chair

The foot of a tripod table from Philadelphia

"the only local cabinetmaker known to have owned one independently was Affleck."[38]

William Wilmerding was a New York merchant who specialized in the importation of looking glasses from England. "Has for sale a large and elegant assortment of gilt and wooden framed Looking Glasses and a variety of other articles of the last importation," ran the language of one advertisement. His shop was listed in city directories from 1789 to 1815. One mirror, with a gilt-scrolled pediment crowned by an exuberant phoenix and centered by a horizontal beaded oval flanked by laurel leaves and attached garlands on the sides, was a favored style for Wilmerding (left). Because so many of these identically designed mirrors have histories of ownership in New York it led Charles Montgomery to speculate that they were made on special order for Wilmerding's shop.[39]

Looking glasses were a cherished form of room decoration. The light-enhancing capabilities of the reflective glass were much appreciated in late eighteenth-century homes where the ability to illuminate a room was always a concern. Many were imported from England because American glassmakers had trouble perfecting the manufacture of high-quality glass plates. Period inventories indicate that looking glasses were used in conjunction with pier tables, and often purchased in pairs. Elbert Haring's New York parlor in 1773 housed "1 Looking Glass and a Table under it," while another New Yorker bequeathed her daughter in 1760, "the two large looking-glasses and the two marble tables which are placed and stand under them."[40] Sophisticated buyers enjoyed the effect of extending the visual line of an interior space by placing two mirrors at opposing, symmetrical wall locations. In 1802, Eliza Southgate Bowne remarked upon visiting the elegantly furnished Salem home of Elias Hasket Derby:

> The moon shown with uncommon splendor. The large marble vases, the images, the mirrors to correspond with the windows, gave it so uniform and finished an appearance, that I could not think it possible I viewed objects that were real, every thing appeared like enchantment.[41] ★

LEFT:
Attributing eighteenth-century looking glasses to either America or England is difficult considering the widespread sale and dispersion of imported English looking glasses throughout the colonies. For example, while a great number of looking glasses have been attributed to William Wilmerding of New York, research has shown that Wilmerding was in fact not a craftsman, but a successful merchant who imported and sold looking glasses, such as the one seen to the left. The architecturally inspired frame is decorated with sparsely carved festoons and scrolled ears crested by a gilded phoenix. Americans resorted to English imports because of an initial difficulty in producing glass plates smooth enough to be silvered. Another frequent practice was the importation of unframed English mirror plates which were embellished with American frames upon arrival.

ABOVE:
Ginger Meyer holding her grandson Jeffrey Christopher Thomas who, at an unusually young age, appears enraptured by this fine Chippendale mahogany wall mirror.

Federal Furniture

In 1790, Archibald Allison remarked in his *Essays on the Nature and Principles of Taste:*

> . . . *Strong and Massy Furniture is everywhere vulgar and unpleasing.*
> *Some years ago every article of furniture was made in what was called the Chinese taste. . . . To this succeeded the Gothic Taste. . . .*
> *The Taste which now reigns is that of the Antique.*
> *Everything we now use is made in imitation of those models which have lately been discovered in Italy.*[1]

During the Revolution, ties with England were temporarily severed, and "material innovations awaited the resumption of commercial, educational, and diplomatic relations with Europe."[2] Afterwards, a new republican awareness crept into the nation's psyche, and Americans looked to ancient Rome and Greece for their models of civic virtue. Classical taste embodied "the promise of perfect beauty and a model of austere patriotism."[3] As one statesman cautioned George Washington in 1790: ". . . everything about you should be substantially good and majestically plain, made to endure."[4]

In Europe, excavations at Herculaneum and Pompeii spawned a reborn appreciation for the cadences of classical design. A stylistic metamorphosis was instigated by the Scottish architect Robert Adam and his brother James when their book, *The Works in Architecture of Robert and James Adam*, was published in London in 1773. It was their endeavor, they wrote, "to seize . . . the beautiful spirit of antiquity, and to transfer it, with novelty and

LEFT:
This fine mahogany serpentine sideboard from New England is prominently featured in the Meyers' dining room. Above it, a carved giltwood and eglomisé wall mirror, probably made in New York, reflects the light of the candles. Also displayed on the sideboard is a porcelain goose tureen, a product of the eighteenth-century Chinese export trade. The swagged urn of flowers and the eglomisé panel on the crest of the mirror, as well as the half-round colonnettes of the frame are all motifs typical of the Federal style.

ABOVE:
The understated elegance of the sideboard is complemented by original shell-brasses which were probably cast in Birmingham, England. The drawers are joined by narrow triangular dovetails which allowed for rich honey-colored mahogany veneers.

ABOVE:
This Federal New York dining chair is one of a rare set of ten decorated with inlaid swag bellflowers on the crest. The design of the back is identical to those on two other sets which may have been crafted by Elbert Anderson, Sr., working in New York City at the very end of the eighteenth century.

variety." They promoted a unity of interior and exterior design, with emphasis upon the abstract geometries of apsidal, circular, elliptical and rectangular patterns, informed by the measure of classical orders.[5] In France, comparable fashions of Louis XVI style gained similar acceptance.

The furniture coming out of this period of neo-classical fashion was later termed "Federal" due to its acceptance during the early years of the republic. The style was characterized by a sleekness and lightness of parts and design motifs. "Good proportions were the byword of real art in Federal cabinet-making. . . ."[6] noted Hornor. Naturalistic carving was supplanted by inlaid patterns of graphically rendered urns, swags, cornucopias, shields, eagles and fruit which were employed because of their moral and allegorical implications. The designs of this period would lead Thomas Sheraton to remark in the 1793 edition of *The Cabinet-Maker and Upholsterer's Drawing Book*:

> *Time alters fashions and frequently obliterates the works of art and ingenuity; but that which is founded on Geometry and real Science, will remain unalterable.*[7]

His book, in addition to two works published in 1788, *The Cabinet-Maker's London Book of Prices*, to which Thomas Shearer heavily contributed, and George Hepplewhite's posthumously published *The Cabinet-Maker and Upholsterer's Guide* outlined the vocabulary of neo-classical style for English and American craftsmen and patrons.

The development of the sideboard, and the notion of a room used exclusively for dining, coincided with the advent of Federal style in America. Previously, the American penchant for maneuverable, open living space meant that meals were taken in general-purpose rooms such as the parlor or sitting room. The birth of the dining room spawned a new modicum of eating etiquette. The affluent appreciated both the conveniences and the theatrical qualities bestowed by a sideboard display. As Hepplewhite remarked: "The great utility of this piece of furniture has procured it a very general reception; and the conveniences it affords render a dining-room incomplete without a sideboard."[8]

The undulant facade of a mahogany sideboard from New England enabled a server to comfortably reach for

The glass doors and shelves on the upper section of this New England desk and bookcase serve as a charming exhibition space for an array of English canary ware and soft-paste pottery from the Meyer collection. The Gothic arches of the mullions and sweeping curves of the cornice complement the latticework backs of the dining chairs.

The three-part mahogany dining table, also from New England, became very popular in the Federal period when large dinner parties were frequent social engagements of the upper and middle classes. The two half-round ends could be used separately for smaller dinner parties, or extended, as seen above, for larger groups.

ABOVE:

A detail of one of the satinwood-inlaid urns above each of the stationary legs of the dining table

ABOVE:
This silhouetted family portrait is signed Auguste Edouart, 1842, Boston, Massachusetts. *Silhouettes were named after Louis XV's minister of finance, Etienne de Silhouette, who was also an amateur portraitist. Auguste Edouart (1789–1861) introduced the French art form to America in 1839 when he emigrated from France. From 1839–1849, Edouart cut silhouettes in Boston,*

Washington, D.C., New Orleans, Philadelphia, Charleston, and New York City. This silhouette has been embellished with a painted background placing the family in a Classical-style drawing room.

BELOW:
An English pottery platter with leaf border and cat in the center

articles set upon the surface (page 70). Noted Sheraton: "If the sideboard be near the entering door of the dining-room, the hollow front will sometimes secure the butler from the jostles of the other servants." Some owners enhanced the presentation of the sideboard by having a recessed cove designed to offset the piece within the room. One observer of a new dining room arrangement declared "an elegant side-board may be classed among its ornaments." Here, the crisp outline of the mahogany facade accented by lightwood inlay, original fan-shaped brasses, and the sleek tapered legs, codify the unit into an elegant statement of neo-classical reserve.

A traveler to Federal America around 1820 reported that in the best homes "there is always a very elegant mahogany side-board decorated with the silver and metal vessels of the household as well as beautiful cut glass and crystal."[9] Candles placed at the back of the serving area thrust light upon the exhibition of these costly wares while mirrors placed above it heightened the illusion of space. The inner compartments of the sideboard included such useful details as: "A drawer in the bottom for a heater," "A celleret drawer on the bottom fitted up for bottles," and "A plate drawer lined with baize." Each variant depended upon the needs and preferences of the owner.[10] Utensils were either housed in an upper

LEFT:
Eagle finial detail of silver coffeepot (see photograph at right)

RIGHT:
This exceptional circa 1800 New York *pembroke table is inlaid with delicate* paterae *and bellflowers. The silver cup made by James Butler (1713–1776) was a gift to Mr. and Mrs. Meyer from Israel Sack. The inked letter reads,* This silver cup—presented by me to Bob and Ginger Meyer on their twenty-fifth wedding anniversary. With my best wishes for continued happiness—Israel Sack. *The lid of the* circa 1805 *silver coffeepot made by Jacob Kucher of Philadelphia is crowned by an eagle finial.*

This circa 1810 two-drawer mahogany work table successfully exhibits the decorative use of contrasting light-and-dark-wood veneers typical of early nineteenth-century northeastern shore New England furniture. The turned ivory knobs on the drawer fronts provide an additional flourish to the case.

drawer or placed in an ornamental cutlery box atop the sideboard.

With new dining practices came an expanded code of dining etiquette. Thomas Sheraton dictated that chairs be placed to allow "2 feet to each person sitting at [the dining] table . . . [for] . . . less than this cannot with comfort be dispensed with."[11] A number of years later, Frances Trollope would remark: "It certainly does not, in my opinion, add to the well ordering of a dinner table, to set the gentlemen at one end of it, and the ladies at the other; but it is very rarely that you find it otherwise."[12]

An unusual set of ten New York chairs features a broken lattice-back and stem from a tradition of furniture with New York lineages (page 72). Two identically fashioned sets, branded with the name "Anderson," have been linked to the Maiden Lane shop of Elbert Anderson, Sr., which he shared with his son, Elbert, Jr., beginning in 1799.[13] The inlay pattern of pendant bellflowers, swags and spandrels which marks the raised crest rail may not be unique to the Anderson shop. Charles Montgomery determined that the "substantial traffic in these charming vignettes and ornamental framing devices . . . [leaves] . . . little doubt that a large proportion of inlays used in the city shops were bought ready made." Cabinetmakers purchased yards of prepared inlay from local suppliers. As a result, identical motifs appear on furniture stemming from various shops located in major cabinetmaking centers.[14]

In pre-Revolutionary American homes, the ritual of dining included moving the table from the wall and returning it there after the meal was through. Born in 1861, the collector Wallace Nutting recalled:

Invariably the dining table was closed and pushed to the wall after every meal, leaving a great empty space of no possible benefit. Our grandmothers would as soon have thought of leaving the dishes unwashed as leaving the table in the floor.

He archly described the practice as one of those "curious instances of the failure of the human mind." It was not until the end of the eighteenth century that families of greater financial means began to maintain one table, positioned in the center of a designated dining space where it came to serve as a symbol of their prestige. The inlaid mahogany dining table from New England offers a good example of the two- and three-sectioned tables that were

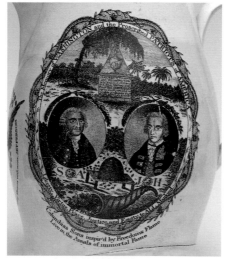

ABOVE:

This rare Queen Anne maple single-drawer tea table from New England displays a variety of accoutrements for an eighteenth-century gentleman. A pipe box inlaid in whalebone with the initials E.H. is accompanied by a long-stemmed clay pipe, wrought-iron pipe tongs, and a tea caddy. The print of Benjamin Franklin is inscribed at the base, D. Martin Pinxt, E. Savage Sculpt.

RIGHT:

Entrepreneurial potters from Liverpool, England, took advantage of America's recent break with her mother country and manufactured graceful baluster-shape cream-colored earthenware decorated with patriotic transfer prints of American heroes such as George Washington and Thomas Jefferson. Very often, pieces were decorated to order for specific patrons, such as a handled jug in the Meyer collection inscribed John and Martha Wheeler, 1771.

FAR LEFT AND LEFT:
This circa 1805 sewing table attributed to John and/or Thomas Seymour of Boston is a tour-de-force of Federal design and artistry, and in its every aspect exhibits the artistic genius of its maker. The top and case are inlaid with an exquisite combination of exotic woods and inlays which are all characteristic of the Boston Federal style. The lunette-inlaid edge of the top borders a veneered mahogany panel and a luminous burled center. The case is supported on exceptionally delicate, reeded, tapered ring-turned legs which terminate in shaped feet and casters. It is clear that the client who ordered this magnificent table requested that it be fitted in the "neatest and most genteel fashion"; the upper drawer is constructed of compartments covered with their original imported gilt-decorated red Moroccan leather lids.

BELOW:
Miniature portraits served both as jewelry and as symbols of affection given in memorial to loved ones. These small oval portraits were typically executed over ivory in opaque watercolor with extraordinary delicacy and precision. For protection they were covered by a hinged oval glass with a metal bezel latch.

designed for neo-classical dining rooms (page 73). The drop-leaf center section, flanked by two D-shaped ends provides swing legs to support the extension leaves. In the words of one etiquette manual, the arrangement of guests around the adjustable surface required "as much thought as a game of chess, for in no way is tact more called into exercise than in the distributing of guests at the dinner table."[15]

The dainty form of a woman's sewing or work table was another piece of specialized furniture popularized during the Federal period. A two-drawer example from Portsmouth, New Hampshire, features a scalloped-edge lower shelf and brilliant panels of mahogany and birch veneer (page 76). There are twenty-two examples of work tables with a similarly designed shelf, which was Portsmouth's answer to the hanging silk bag preferred by many Massachusetts craftsmen (left). Other explicit Portsmouth features include the highly-figured panels of native-wood veneer, the ring-turned legs with a flattened baluster in the upper leg, the midleg reeding, and the elongated foot.[16] In March of 1816, one Portsmouth merchant, Jacob Wendell, ordered a table of similar design from the

cabinetmaking firm of Jonathan Judkins and William Senter for $10. The table was located in the "Back Sitting Room" of his mansion on Pleasant Street.[17]

Compared to the graphic design of the New Hampshire work table, the splashy veneer of the *circa* 1800 Massachusetts sewing table responds more to the table's overall design. The tidy satinwood and maple frame is supported by engaged reeded legs marked by reel turnings. Ownership of such a fancy table bespoke the prestige and leisure time of the women of the house. The upper drawer features Moroccan red-leather-covered compartments for stitching implements such as needles, scissors and thread. The legs are raised on small brass casters which allowed for removal to a favorite work area. As described by New Englander, Margaret Quincy:

> *Mama and I were ready dressed, so descended to the parlour, opened windows, dropped blinds, placed the little table in the middle of the room with work, books, &, &, and seating ourselves on the sopha, Mama held some work, and I read aloud 'Red Gauntlet'. Our preparations were but just concluded, when the gentlemen drove up.*[18]

This elegant example was likely produced by the Creek Square, Boston shop of father and son cabinetmakers, John and Thomas Seymour, who worked in partnership from 1794 to 1804. The elder Seymour was an English-trained craftsman who had settled in Portland, Maine, in 1784 and subsequently moved to Boston in 1794. His furniture designs owed much to the various English pattern books, particularly Hepplewhite and Sheraton. The latter appropriately described a "Table with a Bag used by the Ladies to work at, in which bag they deposit their fancy needlework."[19] A nearly identical table attributed to the Seymours was deemed a "masterpiece" by Albert Sack in *The New Fine Points of Furniture*. It features a lower drawer appointed with the same red leather as the Meyer piece.[20]

The carved posts of an architect's table with a grapevine against a star-punched ground are strongly suggestive of the Salem shop of Samuel McIntire (detail, right). McIntire was a noted architect and carver who crafted a number of the designs for both the interior and exterior of Federal homes in Salem. One of his key clients was the fabulously wealthy Elias Hasket Derby who made

The design for this exquisitely executed architect's table is taken almost directly from plate 30 of Thomas Sheraton's Drawing Book, London, 1793, about which the author writes, "This table will be found highly useful to such as draw, it being designed from my own experience of what is necessary for those who practice this art. The top of this table is made to rise by a double horse, that the designer may stand if he please, or he may sit, and have the top raised to any direction. . . . The sliders at each end are necessary for the instruments of drawing, and for a light to stand on. The long drawer holds paper, square and board, and those drawers which form the kneehole are fitted up for colours."

The attribution of this table to the master carver Samuel McIntire of Salem, Massachusetts, is based in part on the distinctive grape-leaf-carved and punch-work-decorated sections of the upper legs. The Benjamin Franklin-decorated knobs allude to the patriotic inclinations of the original purchaser.

a fortune in international trade due to the liberated atmosphere of free enterprise brought about by the nation's independence, and for whom McIntire fashioned two homes.[21] Although little is known about the size of his shop, the marked similarity of his architectural and furniture carvings has made it possible to identify his hand.

A number of the features of this table are typical of Salem cabinetry—details such as the partially engaged, bulging reeded and tapered legs, the elongated swelled feet and the four turned buttons at the corners to head the posts. The motif of the fertile grapevine well suited the new republican taste and was used repeatedly by McIntire. As a classical symbol of abundance, the bounteous fruit exemplified the rising prosperity of the nation. The brass handholds, imprinted with the profile of a national hero and Renaissance man, Benjamin Franklin, confirm that the original owner must have been as concerned with the patriotic inferences of the decorative motifs as he was with the ingenuity of the complex table design. ★

A Portsmouth, New Hampshire, Flame Birch-Veneered Bureau

The design of this chest is derived from Plate 76 of George Hepplewhite's *The Cabinet-Maker and Upholsterer's Guide* (third edition, 1794). Simply termed "Dressing Drawers" by the stylist, it featured four drawers contained within a bowed-front frame with "French feet and a scalloped skirt with central drop." Hepplewhite advised that the top drawer be used for "the necessary dressing equipage, the others are applicable to common uses."[1]

The drop-panel motif is one which is derived from the earlier rococo impulse to adorn the apron with a carved shell or fan detail. Here, compartmentalized panels of diagonally-cut mahogany and birch veneer embody the Portsmouth craftsman's enthusiasm for the spirit of neo-classical geometries. The cabinetmaker chose to counterbalance the horizontal thrust of the drawers with a cascade of oval ornamentation down the central panel, terminating in the low drop. Five other examples of Portsmouth bow-front chests with drop panels have been identified with a similar oval rather than rectangular pattern.[2]

At the start of the nineteenth century, Portsmouth experienced a commercial boom. The rapid growth of the seaport attracted craftsmen from nearby towns as well as the more removed urban centers of Boston, Salem and Newburyport in Massachusetts. Portsmouth merchants had developed a unique "trading niche" along the northeast coast. With timber as their mainstay, they fostered strong ties with the West Indies, Newfoundland and northern Europe in addition to more established markets in Great Britain and southern Europe. The success of their ventures can be measured by the ambitiously designed furnishings that they purchased in the neo-classical mode. The flamboyance of this chest of drawers well suited a town which was described by one visitor as having gone "beyond most others . . . in their sumptuous and elegant living."[3]

Strongly contrasting light and dark inlay is typical of Portsmouth cabinetmaking. In this superb example, the facade is decorated with a central tier of birch oval inlay flanked by tiers of rectangular inlays. The oval inlay is extended to the central drop panel of the skirt, an innovation which has led Brock Jobe, a scholar of Portsmouth cabinetmaking, to celebrate the cabinetmaker for having "raised the drop-panel to its highest level." Another unique ornament is the curving sweep of the French feet, which is usually spurred at the juncture with the skirt. The hen-and-chick brasses can be found on other chests of this unique group of six. A forthcoming book published by Winterthur will illustrate this motif designed by the Birmingham Brass Foundry in England.

1. Diane Carlberg Ehrenpreis, in *Portsmouth Furniture: Masterworks from the New Hampshire Seacoast*, organized and edited by Brock Jobe (Boston: Society for the Preservation of New England Antiquities, 1993), p. 112.
2. Ehrenpreis, in *Portsmouth Furniture*, pp. 114–116.
3. Johanna McBrien, in *Portsmouth Furniture: Masterworks from the New Hampshire Seacoast*, organized and edited by Brock Jobe (Boston: Society for the Preservation of New England Antiquities, 1993), p. 65; and for further discussion of Portsmouth's economic development see pp. 58–70.

Folk and Decorative Art and Furniture

The story has been told that George I of England was caught in a thunderstorm one day and sought shelter in the home of a commoner. As he warmed himself by the fire, he was offered a seat in a chair crafted almost completely of spindles. He was amazed by the simple comfort of the form. Upon his return to Windsor Castle, he ordered several to be made, and thus the term "Windsor Chair" was born.[1]

Though that particular slice of Windsor chair history may be apocryphal, in America, Windsor-like chairs derived from English examples were first made in Philadelphia around 1740.[2] By the 1790s, the bow-backed Windsor side chair had become "the principal vernacular chair throughout America."[3] In Philadelphia it spawned a veritable cottage industry as craftsmen met enormous success exporting these versatile seats to other American cities, particularly in the coastal South. "We have a Windsor chairmaker next door to us, who I think, by the smell, is boiling varnish this day," remarked Philadelphia diarist Elizabeth Drinker on June 24, 1806.[4] A traveler from London in 1800 reported: "It is scarcely possible to go one mile on this road without meeting numbers of waggons passing and repassing between the back parts of the state and Philadelphia." He continued by noting that Philadelphia's trade extended "as far as Pittsburgh itself, which is on the Ohio, with the back of Virginia, and, strange to tell, with Kentucky, seven hundred miles distant."[5]

The form of the Windsor chair was conducive to speculative marketing practices. Prices of chairs were lowered as chairmakers were able to turn out hundreds of legs and stretchers in expectation of later sales. Americans utilized the structural properties of native woods and were able to improve upon the heavier, "overengineered English

LEFT:
The Meyers' keeping room is decorated with furniture and decorations in the Folk tradition. Note the carved eagle by German immigrant Wilhelm Schimmel on top of the cupboard and the polychrome-painted lidded 'bucher' boxes. The green-painted fan-back Windsor chair is one of a pair stamped I. Henzey. *A detail of the stamp can be seen below.*

This brand, reading I Henzey, *is found on the underside of a pair of fan-back Windsor chairs, one of which is seen on the facing page. Joseph Henzey (b. 1743) worked at 106 South Eighth Street and 76 Almond Street in Philadelphia producing high-quality Windsor chairs in the late eighteenth century. Some of his commissions were sets of Windsor chairs ordered by the Library Company, the State Assembly, and the First Bank of America.*

ABOVE:
Among the artistic achievements of the young girls who attended private schools and academies in the early nineteenth century, are a variety of "theorem," or stencil paintings executed over silk, canvas and velvet, an example of which can be seen above. The girls arranged pieced stencil designs, usually of fruit, birds and flowers, into still life paintings, the hallmark achievement of an accomplished young lady.

*Rhode Island Windsors such as this
example, one of a pair, are characterized
by strongly profiled leg turnings of compressed balusters and a highly defined
overlapping ring at the center of the leg.
The taper at the base of the bottle-shaped
leg is also typical of Windsor chairs from
this region.*

Windsor."[6] Strong woods such as oak, hickory or ash
were used for the bow-back crest and spindles, softer
woods such as white pine or tulip-poplar for the seat, and
maple for the lathe-turned legs and armrests. Ideally
made without nails, the spindles and legs could later be
fitted into a seat of unseasoned wood, and as the wood
dried, it tightened on the spindles and legs, securing their
position.[7] Most often, a coat of green, blue, red or black
paint served to unify the whole and mask the melange of
wood types.

One bow-backed Windsor chair descended in the
Rogers family of Rhode Island (left). A label on the under-
neath explains that the chair was originally owned by
John Rogers, and that, "It was his parlour chair, and the
Generals of that war sat in it" (detail, right). Rogers was a
descendant of James Rogers, "an inhabitant of Newport,
as early as 1638," and who may have been a son of
Thomas Rogers, "of the Mayflower." During the war,
John Rogers rose to the rank of Captain, and "was several
times a representative in the Colonial Assembly."[8]

At the time of the Revolution, one Providence chairmaker advertised:

> *All kinds of Windsor chairs . . . in the newest and best
> Fashions, neat, elegant and strong, beautifully painted,
> after the Philadelphia mode, warranted of good sea-
> soned Materials, so firmly put together as not to
> deceive the Purchasers by an untimely coming to
> pieces.*[9]

Indeed, the Windsor mode was built to withstand both
indoor and outdoor use. In 1774, The First Continental
Congress meeting at Carpenter's Hall in Philadelphia sat
upon Windsor armchairs. And in 1794, George
Washington ordered 27 bow-back Windsor chairs to be
used "on the portico of his Mount Vernon home."
However, usage was not limited to the new republican
leaders. The affordable Windsor chair proved to be the
quintessential, democratic seat as shown by its location in
the Rogers parlor as well as in other American households
of varying economic means.[10]

As professional craftsmen continued to develop their
techniques, another group of artisans created a body of
vernacular or folk pieces for a different sort of audience.
Folk art generally refers to the body of work crafted by
untutored, everyday people who made effective use of

available resources to create unique visions that were highly reflective of popular culture. Wilhelm Schimmel was one such craftsman (1817–90). Soon after the Civil War, Schimmel, a native of Hesse-Darmstadt, Germany, embarked upon a nomadic existence, traveling around the western Pennsylvania countryside in the Cumberland Valley near Carlisle. He stayed in the area until his death some twenty years later, doing odd jobs for other German residents, and selling or trading carved biblical figures, toys, animals and birds, for food and lodging.

Schimmel's approach never advanced beyond the pocket knife. Most of his pieces were chiseled from soft pine, treated with gesso (plaster) and then painted. A chip-

This chair belonged to John Rogers, COL. John Rogers great, great Grand father. At the time of the Revolution. It was his parlor chair, and the Generals of that war sat in it.

carved eagle with brown and black feathers "cross-hatched" along its broad wing spread is typical of his designs and may be derived from the Hapsburg eagles of his homeland (page 89). Most often, the wings and body were crafted separately and then doweled or mortised.[11] Schimmel was poor and plagued by alcoholism, but he was a notable figure in the Cumberland Valley. His obituary from the Carlisle *Evening Sentinel* of August 7 reported:

> *'Old Schimmel', the German who for many years tramped through this and adjoining counties, died at the Almshouse on Sunday. His only occupation was carving heads of animals out of soft pine wood. . . .*[12]

The definition of folk art can be extended to include the theorem paintings, embroideries and japanned and painted boxes created at home or in school academies by young women. A theorem painting on velvet of a basket of fruit being preyed upon by two humming birds offers a typical example of an academy assignment (page 84). The "theory" behind its painting involved the formation of a pattern, with the aid of a stencil, which was then artfully colored and toned with oil paint. The eloquent

The circa 1795 continuous-arm Windsor chair seen in detail on the opposite page, is displayed in front of a rare Queen Anne painted maple desk-on-frame. On the underside of the saddle seat is a label which places this chair and its mate in the home of John Rogers, a colonel in the American Revolution. The appearance of Windsor chairs in a number of late eighteenth-century portraits of wealthy American merchants and statesmen, as well as of the common man, indicates the wide appeal and manufacture of Windsor chairs.

Joined chests, painted with symbolic motifs, were a prolific art of the Pennsylvania-Germans. This example, inscribed and dated 1793 by John Seltzer (1744–1845) of Jonestown, Pennsylvania, characteristically depicts two panels with five tulips in a tankard, painted over a white ground. Although such imagery was a popular symbol of the resurrection and regeneration of Christ, Benno Forman, a celebrated art historian, notes as motifs were passed from generation to generation, they became simply decorative rather than symbolically associative.

Wilhelm Schimmel (1817–1890) was a German-born artisan who came to America after the Civil War where he led a peripatetic life in Pennsylvania, selling and trading his chip-carved sculpture for room and board or tavern refreshments. Although Schimmel sculpted a variety of animals and birds, he is perhaps best known for his eagles, carved with a jack-knife and decorated with brightly colored polychrome paints. They range in wingspan from eight inches to over thirty inches.

completion of such a work showcased the facility of the artist's hand as well as her fashion aptitude. Other appropriately genteel themes involved scenes from mythology, the bible, history or literature. The marked similarity among many of these works, implies that they were derived from common design sources such as prints, magazines and illustrated Bibles.

The sociological implications of seminary art were far more complex than the designs. The academies for girls hammered home the notion that the finesse with which a young woman completed her assignments bore strong implications as to her future dexterity in household supervision. Furthermore, her accomplishments reflected equally upon a young woman's talents and upon her family's ability to educate her in the proper manner. The pressure to perform is revealed in the following ditty from 1820:

The colour'd Sampler's work displays
The stitch and mark in various ways,
For ev'ry observer's tongue to praise
THE SCHOOL GIRL! [13]

The painted and japanned lids of eight decorative boxes demonstrate another female accomplishment taught by men such as Lawrence Smith, "Drawing Master, of Trenton, N.J.," who advertised in the *Republican and Savannah Evening Ledger* in 1811, "that fashionable style of ornamenting ladies dressing boxes, Tables &c." (four shown on page 90). The technique was explained in the fittingly titled, *Handmaid to the Arts* (London, 1758):

By japanning is here to be understood the art of covering bodies by grounds of opake colours in varnish;

Two nineteenth-century decorated tole-ware coffeepots from Pennsylvania

Polychrome-painted boxes, like theorem paintings, were most often decorated by female students attending nineteenth-century academies. They were very personal objects used for the storage of small possessions. Most girls signed and dated their boxes.

A circa 1785 serpentine-top card table from Rhode Island is an elegant centerpiece for the display of early nineteenth-century painted wooden boxes and a wallpaper-covered hatbox from the Meyer collection. The hatbox below the table is covered with wallpaper depicting a chapel and buildings. Hatboxes, or bandboxes, found wide appeal among women who entered the growing industrial labor force of the early nineteenth century. The boxes served as lightweight luggage and storage for hats, collars, and ribbons, as they commuted from their rural homes to the urban industrial centers.

which may be either afterwards, decorated by paintings or gilding, or left in a plain state. . . . The substances which admit of being japanned are almost every kind that are dry and rigid, or not too flexible: as wood, metals, leather, and paper prepared.[14]

The beginnings of a philosophical shift with regard to women's education are revealed in an editorial in *The Boston Weekly Magazine and Ladies' Miscellany* of February 28, 1818:

The design of the present fashionable system of education for females, appears to be to bestow upon young ladies such temporary accomplishments as make them showy girls rather than useful women. . . .[15]

A disparate branch of folk art stemmed from the decorative arts crafted by many of the German immigrants from the Rhine Valley and parts of Switzerland and Holland, who had emigrated to America and settled in the southeastern part of William Penn's religiously tolerant Pennsylvania. These Pennsylvania Germans had farming backgrounds and sought to continue their ways in the areas of Lancaster and Berks counties which were later redefined to include Lebanon, Dauphin, Northumberland,

and Schuylkill counties. They were predominantly Lutherans and members of the German Reformed Church "although Moravians and the pietistic sects such as Amish, Mennonites, and Schwenkfelderes" settled there as well.[16] With religion as their cornerstone, they gathered in loosely organized communities which shared churches and schools and perpetuated the furniture forms, architecture and decorative arts of their homeland on American soil.

The rectangular form of the Pennsylvania-German chest was derived from German and Swiss designs of the late Middle Ages. It was usually constructed of six planks of white pine or tulip-poplar and dovetailed together. Most chests opened with a lift-top and were used to house clothing and textiles which were laid out flat in the belly of the piece. The precious nature of fabric goods during the colonial era cannot be overemphasized because, "the production of linen, for example, took at least a year from planting to sewing."[17] To the left of the chest's interior, a small built-in container called a till, a device dating to German designs of the fifteenth century, served for the storage of small valuables. Used by both men and women, the chests were sometimes acquired as personal treasures "before the time of marriage."[18]

One such chest painted with tulip flowers and tankards, both symbols of hospitality and domesticity, is signed "John Seltzer" and dated "1793" (page 88). Seltzer, his father Christian, and two neighbors in the Rank family, were part of a small school of woodworkers who signed and dated the pieces they constructed in Jonestown, Lebanon county. The will of an older sibling, Christian, Jr., referred to John as a "House Carpenter," while John's estate inventory, taken on February 6, 1845, included "a lot of Boards," "Plaining bench & carpenter tools," "chisel," "woodsaw" and "6 axes."[19] Both statements underscore the flexible nature of his handicraft.

One might think that the inventiveness of early American craftsmen was hampered by a limited selection of tools, and that the pieces they produced were remarkable considering the technological restraints. However, by the eighteenth century, the tools that were used were the product of centuries of aesthetic and technological experimentation. For instance, the advent of the dovetail led to the creation of "thinner and finer-toothed saws and the refinement of specialized planes for cutting joints." The width of a molding plane determined the size of the groove it cut and thereby established consistency within a craftsman's output (below). Woods were chosen not only for decorative appeal, but for maneuverability and carvability.[20]

Furniture connoisseurship demands an understanding of such details. As historian Benno Forman once remarked:

> Many collectors of American furniture profess no interest in tools and the ways in which they were used, a curiously self-defeating attitude, since a knowledge of hand tools, the marks that they make, and the ways in which they could be used are better insurance against making a collecting error than all the books on art ever published.

Indeed, the markings left behind by the tools and hand of the craftsman are witness to the flavor and intent of each piece. As Forman further noted: "To the colonial craftsman the adage 'Time is money' had a grimly serious meaning." The ability of an artisan to work quickly was part and parcel of his success, and "a craftsman did not lavish workmanship on the parts of his furniture that were not visible."[21] Thus, the nature of a piece's handi-

LEFT AND BELOW:
A selection of woodworking tools given to Adolph Meyer by his father

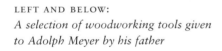

ABOVE:
The circa 1795 Windsor youth's chair appears to retain its original green paint. The red-stained New England birchwood candlestand has exceptionally delicate proportions and is displayed beneath a watercolor depicting a basket of flowers which was probably made in New England during the first quarter of the nineteenth century.

Adolph H. Meyer

craft is often revealed on the underneaths of drawers, the backs of case pieces and in the refinement of the dovetailing. As James M. Gaynor, a historian of mechanical arts has written: "Few other artifacts have the power to so intimately connect us with the men who used them or enhance our understanding of the furniture they made."[22]

Adolph H. Meyer was the son of a German immigrant craftsman who instilled in him at an early age a keen awareness of individuality expressed through artisanship, well before he became an industrial magnate. As he focused upon his passion for Americana, Mr. Meyer never lost sight of his father's insights and instincts. He lingered over the nuances of handicraft as defined by color, pattern and construction techniques. He experimented with a selection of antique tools to enhance his knowledge of various crafts (page 92). He worked with like-minded dealers such as Jess Pavey, whose concern for quality, integrity and authenticity is legendary; and Israel Sack, who devised a collecting strategy that distinguished between the "good, better, and best" pieces, that proved a maxim for Mr. Meyer's own collecting goals. With these goals in mind, the Meyers established the Americana Foundation, and their appreciation of fine Americana continues through succeeding generations of the Meyer family.

It is not surprising, then, that during the course of his forty-some-odd years of collecting, Mr. Meyer acquired the Philadelphia arm chair, previously owned by Walpole Society member Dwight Blaney (page 45); or, that the Thomas Affleck "French" chair, already a rarity when it was bespoke by Joseph Wharton, Sr., over two centuries ago, should have caught his eye as an expression of simple elegance (page 64); or, that the neo-Palladian secretary once owned by Revolutionary stalwart and man of letters, Jonathan Jackson, similarly titillated Mr. Meyer's fascination with American heroes (page 37). A fellow Walpolean once remarked of Blaney's assemblage of antiques: "This was not an aggregation, but a collection of which each piece was known and loved."[23] The same words well describe the scope and breadth and heart of the Adolph H. Meyer Collection which so completely recognizes the development of woodworking artisanship in America. ★

Endnotes

Seventeenth Century Furniture

1. William Wood, *New England's Prospect*, ed. by E. M. Boynton (1634; reprint, Boston, 1897), pp. 16–18, as quoted in Benno M. Forman, *American Seating Furniture, 1630–1730: An Interpretive Catalogue* (New York: W.W. Norton, 1988), p. 20.
2. Francis Higginson, as quoted in Marshall B. Davidson, *The American Heritage History of American Antiques from the Revolution to the Civil War* , 3 vols. (New York: American Heritage Publishing, 1967), I: 9.
3. Forman, *Seating Furniture*, p. 40.
4. Brock Jobe and Myrna Kaye, *New England Furniture: The Colonial Era* (Boston: Houghton, Mifflin, 1984), p. 3.
5. John Fleming and Hugh Honor, *Dictionary of the Decorative Arts* (New York: Harper & Row Publishers, 1977), p. 808.
6. Christopher P. Monkhouse and Thomas S. Michie, *American Furniture in Pendleton House* (Providence, R.I.: Museum of Art, Rhode Island School of Design, 1986), 144.
7. [Samuel Sewall,] Diary of Samuel Sewall, 1674–1729, ed. M. Halsey Thomas, 2 vols. (New York: Farrar, Straus, and Giroux, 1973), 2:839, as quoted in Forman, *Seating Furniture*, p. 84.
8. Harold Sack and Deanne Levison, "Queen Anne and Chippendale Armchairs in America," *Antiques* 137 (May 1990), 1166.
9. Monkhouse and Michie, 147.
10. Davidson, I: 76.
11. Samuel Sewall, "Letter-Book of Samuel Sewall, Vol. II," *Collections of the Massachusetts Historical Society*, 6th ser., 2 (1888): 839, as quoted in Forman, "The Chest of Drawers," p. 15.
12. Edgar de N. Mayhew and Minor Myers, Jr., *A Documentary History of American Interiors: From the Colonial Era to 1915* (New York: Charles Scribner's Sons, 1980), p. 29.
13. Forman, "Chest of Drawers," p. 15.
14. Robert F. Trent, "The Symonds Shops of Essex County, Massachusetts," in *The American Craftsman and the European Tradition 1620–1820*, ed. Francis J. Puig and Michael Conforti (Minneapolis: The Minneapolis Institute of Arts, 1989), 32.
15. Trent, "Symonds," pp. 27–8.
16. Forman, "Chest of Drawers," p. 16.
17. William M. Hornor, Jr., *Blue Book: Philadelphia Furniture* (1935; reprint, Washington, D.C.: Highland House, 1977), p. 29.

Queen Anne Furniture

1. Edwin J. Hipkiss in *The Notable American Collection of Mr. and Mrs. Norvin H. Green*, November 29–30, December 1–2, 1950 (New York: Parke-Bernet Galleries, 1950), foreword.
2. Robert F. Trent, "The Colchester School of Cabinetmaking, 1750–1800," in *The American Craftsman and the European Tradition 1620-1820*, ed. Francis J. Puig and Michael Conforti (Minneapolis: The Minneapolis Institute of Arts, 1989), 112.
3. Charles F. Montgomery and Patricia E. Kane, eds., "A Display of American Art, 1750–1800: Furniture" in *American Art: 1750–1800 Towards Independence* (Boston: New York Graphic Society, 1976), 145.
4. Jonathan L. Fairbanks and Elizabeth Bidwell Bates, *American Furniture: 1620 to the Present* (New York: Richard Marek, 1981), p. 86.
5. Montgomery and Kane, "A Display of Art," 144.
6. Monkhouse and Michie, 132.
7. Joseph Downs, *American Furniture: Queen Anne and Chippendale* (New York: McMillan, 1952), 302.
8. Elisabeth Donaghy Garrett, *At Home: The American Family, 1750–1870* (New York: Harry N. Abrams, Inc., 1989), p. 124.
9. Forman, *Seating Furniture*, p. 357.
10. Morrison H. Heckscher, *In Quest of Comfort: The Easy Chair in America* (New York: The Metropolitan Museum of Art, 1971), p. 10.
11. Garrett, *At Home*, p. 230.
12. Jane C. Nylander, *Our Own Snug Fireside: Images of the New England Home, 1760–1860* (New Haven: Yale University Press, 1994), p. 28.
13. Nicholas B. Wainwright, *Colonial Grandeur in Philadelphia: The House and Furniture of General John Cadwalader* (Philadelphia: The Historical Society of Pennsylvania, 1964), pp. 42, 102.
14. Mark Anderson and Robert F. Trent, "A Catalogue of American Easy Chairs" in *American Furniture 1993*, ed. Luke Beckerdite (Hanover, N.H.: University Press of New England for the Chipstone Foundation, 1993), p. 219.
15. *The Collection of Mr. and Mrs. Eddy G. Nicholson*, January 27 and 28, 1995 (New York: Christie's, 1995), lot 1062.
16. Forman, *Seating Furniture*, p. 358.
17. Michael Moses, *Master Craftsmen of Newport: The Townsends and Goddards* (Tenafly, N.J.: By the author, 1984), p. 9.
18. Moses, p. 9.
19. Harold Sack, "The Development of the American High Chest of Drawers," *Antiques* 132 (May 1988), 1119.
20. Moses, p. 9.
21. John Fannig. Watson, *Annals of Philadelphia* (Philadelphia: Hunt, 1830), p. 184; in Mayhew and Myers, p. 60.
22. Garrett, *At Home*, p. 127.
23. Montgomery and Kane, "A Display of Art," 146.
24. Monkhouse and Michie, 165.
25. Piero Rebora, comp., *Cassell's Italian Dictionary* (New York: Macmillan, 1967), p. 87.
26. Monkhouse and Michie, 165.
27. Morrison H. Heckscher, "Philadelphia Furniture, 1760–90: Native-Born and London-Trained Craftsmen" in *The American Craftsman and the European Tradition 1620–1820*, ed. Francis J. Puig and Michael Conforti (Minneapolis: The Minneapolis Institute of Arts, 1989), p. 93.
28. Thomas Sheraton, *The Cabinet Dictionary* (London: N. Smith, King Street, 1803), p. 302; in Charles F. Montgomery, *American Furniture: The Federal Period* (New York: Viking, 1966), p. 243.
29. Thomas Sheraton, *The Cabinet-Maker and Upholsterer's Drawing Book* (1793; reprint, New York: Dover, 1972), p. 114.
30. Nylander, pp. 106–107.
31. Garrett, *At Home*, p. 150.
32. Monkhouse and Michie, 62.
33. John T. Kirk, *Early American Furniture* (New York: Alfred A. Knopf, 1981), p. 16.
34. Morrison H. Heckscher, *American Furniture in The Metropolitan Museum of Art: Late Colonial Period, the Queen Anne and Chippendale Styles* (New York: Random House, 1985), p. 209.
35. As quoted in Abbott Lowell Cummings, *Rural Household Inventories: Establishing the Names, Uses and Furnishings of Rooms in the Colonial New England Home, 1675–1775* (Boston: The Society for the Preservation of New England Antiquities, 1964), p. 191; and Wainwright, *Colonial Grandeur*, pp. 72–73; in Nancy Goyne Evans, "The Bureau Table in America" in *Winterthur Portfolio III*, ed. Ian M. G. Quimby (Winterthur, Del.: Henry Francis du Pont Winterthur Museum, 1967), pp. 35–36.

Chippendale Furniture

1. Morrison H. Heckscher and Leslie Greene Bowman, *American Rococo, 1750–1775: Elegance in Ornament* (New York: Harry N. Abrams, 1992), pp. 1–3.
2. Montgomery and Kane, "A Display of Art," 144.
3. Hornor, p. 70.
4. Hornor, p. 98.
5. Davidson, II: 20.
6. Rodris Roth, "Tea Drinking in 18th Century America: Its Etiquette and Equipage" (Washington, D.C.: Smithsonian, 1961), Paper 14, p. 67.
7. Hornor, p. 147.
8. Hornor, p. 141.
9. David L. Barquist, *American Tables and Looking Glasses* (New Haven, Conn.: Yale University Art Gallery, 1992), p. 232.
10. Hornor, p. 141.
11. Hornor, p. 142.
12. Hornor, p. 90.
13. Heckscher, "Philadelphia Furniture," p. 95.
14. Elizabeth Stillinger, *The Antiquers* (New York: Alfred A. Knopf, 1980), p. 165.
15. Stillinger, pp. 105–106.
16. Stillinger, p. 109.
17. Thomas Sheraton, in Horner, p. 138.
18. Hornor, p. 139.
19. Montgomery and Kane, "A Display of Art," p. 160.
20. Trent, "Colchester," pp. 112–113.
21. Trent, "Colchester," p. 117.
22. Trent, "Colchester," pp. 115–117, 126.
23. Gerald W. R. Ward, "Avarice and Conviviality: Card Playing In Federal America," *Antiques* 141 (May 1992), 795.
24. Wainwright, pp. 72–73.
25. Barquist, p. 164.
26. Moses, p. 13.
27. Barquist, p. 164.
28. Hornor, p. 112.
29. Hornor, p. 114.
30. Ephraim Chambers, *Cyclopaedia; or, An Universal Dictionary of Arts and Sciences* (London, 1783), as quoted in Garrett, *At Home*, p. 128.
31. Barquist, p. 195.
32. Hornor, p. 114.
33. Heckscher, *Queen Anne and Chippendale*, p. 118.
34. Hornor, Pl. 269.
35. Anne Hollingsworth Wharton, *Genealogy of the Wharton Family of Philadelphia, 1664–1880* (Philadelphia: Collins, 1880), p. 101.
36. Wharton, p. 102.
37. Hornor, Pl. 269.
38. Heckscher, *Queen Anne and Chippendale*, p. 118.
39. Charles F. Montgomery, *American Furniture: The Federal Period* (New York: Viking, 1966), Pl. 212, p. 260.
40. Sarah Anna Emery, *Reminiscences of a Nonagenarian* (1879; reprint, Bowie, Md., and Hampton, N.C.: Heritage Books, 1978), p. 244; in Elisabeth Donaghy Garrett, "Looking Glasses in America 1700–1850"; in Barquist, p. 28.
41. Eliza Southgate Bowne, *A Girl's Life Eighty Years Ago: Selections from the Letters of Eliza Southgate Bowne* (New York: Charles Scribner's Sons, 1887), p. 113; in Garrett, "Looking Glasses," in Barquist, p. 34.

Federal Furniture

1. Montgomery, *Federal Period*, p. 9.
2. Hornor, p. 232.
3. Wendy Cooper, *Classical Taste in America, 1800–1840* (New York: Abbeville Press, 1993), p. 15.
4. Montgomery, "A Display of Art," 171.
5. Wayne Craven, *American Art: History and Culture* (New York: Harry N. Abrams, Inc., 1994), p. 115.
6. Hornor, p. 250.
7. Thomas Sheraton, *The Cabinet-Maker and Upholsterer's Drawing-Book* (1802; reprint, New York: Praeger Publishers, 1970), frontispiece; in Montgomery and Kane, "A Display of Art," 171.
8. Deanne Levison and Harold Sack, "Identifying Regionalism in Sideboards: A Study of Documented Tapered-Leg Examples," *Antiques* 141 (May 1992), 821.
9. Thomas Sheraton, *The Cabinet-Maker and Upholsterer's Drawing-Book*, 3d ed. (1802; New York, 1970), p. 366; Robert Kerr, *The Gentleman's House; or, How to Plan English Residences, from the Parsonage to the Palace . . .* (2d ed., London: John Murray, 1865), p. 93; in Garrett, *At Home*, pp. 87–89.
10. *Journeyman's Book of Prices*, in Hornor, p. 261.
11. Thomas Sheraton, *Cabinet Dictionary*, p. 199; in Gerald W. R. Ward, "The Intersection of Life: Tables and Their Social Role"; in Barquist, p. 18.
12. Frances M. Trollope, *Domestic Manners of the Americans*, ed. Donald Smalley (1832; New York, 1949), p. 299; in Garrett, *At Home*, p. 85.
13. Levison and Sack, "Sideboards," 829.
14. Montgomery, *Federal Period*, p. 40.
15. Wallace Nutting, in Ward, "Intersection of Life," in Barquist, pp. 22–23; and Mrs. H. O. Ward, *Sensible Etiquette of the Best Society*, 10th ed. (Philadelphia: Porter and Coates, 1878), pp. 159–160, in Ward, "Intersection of Life," in Barquist, p. 20.
16. Diane Carlberg Ehrenpreis, in *Portsmouth Furniture: Masterworks from the New Hampshire Seacoast*, organized and edited by Brock Jobe (Boston: Society for the Preservation of New England Antiquities, 1993), p. 271.
17. Gerald W. R. Ward and Karin E. Cullity, "The Wendell Family Furniture at Strawbery Banke Museum" in *American Furniture 1993*, ed. Luke Beckerdite (Hanover, N.H.: University Press of New England for the Chipstone Foundation, 1993), p. 249.
18. M. A. De Wolfe Howe, *The Articulate Sisters*, ed.Wolfe (Cambridge: Harvard University Press, 1946), p. 66; in Montgomery, *Federal Furniture*, p. 398.
19. Montgomery, *Federal Period*, p. 397.
20. Albert Sack, *The New Fine Points of Furniture: Early American* (New York: Crown Publishers, 1993), p. 308.
21. Montgomery and Kane, "A Display of Art," 171.

Folk and Decorative Art and Furniture

1. Charles Santore, *The Windsor Style in America* (Philadelphia: Running Press, 1981), p. 31.
2. Charles F. Montgomery, "Regional Preferences and Characteristics in American Decorative Arts: 1750–1800," in *American Art: 1750–1800 Towards Independence*, ed. Charles F. Montgomery and Patricia E. Kane (Boston: New York Graphic Society, 1976), p. 61.
3. Nancy Goyne Evans, "Design Transmission in Vernacular Seating Furniture: The influence of Philadelphia and Baltimore Styles on Chairmaking from the Chesapeake Bay to the 'West'," in *American Furniture 1993*, ed. Luke Beckerdite (Hanover, N.H.: University Press of New England for the Chipstone Foundation, 1993), p. 77.
4. Elizabeth Drinker, *Extracts from the Journal of Elizabeth Drinker, from 1759 to 1807 A.D.*, ed. Henry D. Biddle (Philadelphia, 1889), p. 401; in Garrett, *At Home*, p. 256.
5. Isaac Weld, *Travels through the States of North America*, 2 vols. (London: John Stockdale, 1800), I: 59, 115; in Evans, "Design Transmission," p. 75.
6. Montgomery, "Regional Preferences," p. 61.
7. Carla Mathes Woodward and Franklin W. Robinson, eds., *A Handbook of the Museum of Art, Rhode Island School of Design* (Providence, R.I.: Rhode Island School of Design, 1985), 320–321.
8. *Representative Men and Old Families of Rhode Island: Genealogical Records and Historical Sketches of Prominent and Representative Citizens and Many of the Old Families*, vol. 1 (Chicago: J. H. Beers and Co., 1908), p. 120.
9. Hornor, p. 308.
10. Santore, p. 29.
11. Beatrix T. Rumford and Carolyn J. Weekley, *Treasures of American Folk Art from the Abby Aldrich Rockefeller Folk Art Center* (Boston: Little, Brown and Company, 1989), pp. 205–206.
12. Rumford and Weekley, p. 208.
13. "Shewing the Sampler," from William Upton, *The School-Girl in 1820* (London, 1820), engraving, in Davida Tenenbaum Deutsch, "The Polite Lady: Portraits of American Schoolgirls and Their Accomplishments, 1725–1830," *Antiques* 135 (March 1989), 747.
14. Laurence Smith as quoted in (*Republican and Savannah Evening Ledger*, November 28, 1811 [in the file of the Museum of Early Southern Decorative Arts]); and [Robert Dossie's] *Handmaid to the Arts* (London, 1758), vol. 1, pp. 406–407; in Deutsch, 749.
15. *The Boston Weekly Magazine and Ladies' Miscellany*, February 28, 1811; in Deutsch, 749.
16. Dean A. Fales, Jr., *American Painted Furniture, 1660–1880* (New York: E. P. Dutton, 1972), p. 447.
17. Beatrice B. Garvan and Charles F. Hummel, *The Pennsylvania Germans: A Celebration of Their Arts. 1683–1850* (Philadelphia: Philadelphia Museum of Art, 1982), p. 15.
18. Monroe H. Fabien, *The Pennsylvania-German Decorated Chest* (New York: Universe Books, 1978), p. 28.
19. Fabien, p. 65.
20. James M. Gaynor, "Woodworking Tools in Early America," *Antiques* 145 (May 1994), 717–718.
21. Forman, *Seating Furniture*, p. 46.
22. Gaynor, p. 723.
23. Stillinger, p. 109.